Training Dogs the Aussie Way

A PRACTICAL GUIDE FOR DOG OWNERS BY THE FOUNDERS OF THE WORLD'S LARGEST DOG TRAINING COMPANY

Danny and Sylvia Wilson

Foreword by Andrew Brooke and Liam Crowe

StarJunction Books,
a division of StarJunction International, Inc.

This book's imprint is a registered trademark of StarJunction Books, a division of StarJunction International, Inc.

Important note: The training techniques used in this book should be practiced with safety in mind, as well as the safety of your dog and other people. The authors and publisher accept no responsibility for any loss, damage, injury, or inconvenience sustained by any person or pet as a result of using the methods outlined herein.

Training Dogs the Aussie Way by Sylvia and Danny Wilson

First Edition, August 2007
Copyright © 2007 by Sylvia and Danny Wilson, Bark Busters Home Dog Training.
All rights reserved.

Cover photography by Donna Ryan
Cover design by Gary Mason
Interior design by Brenn Lea Pearson
Illustrations by Emily J. Marino
Copyright © 2007 All rights reserved.

Reviewers: Cathy Drier, Anne George, Donna Ryan, and Jeanne Williams
Editors: Karen Conway, Sandra Fischer, Liam Crowe, and Bill Marino

StarJunction Books trade paperback: ISBN 978-0-9790956-1-0

The Library of Congress has catalogued this edition as follows:

Wilson, Sylvia and Danny, Training Dogs the Aussie Way
ISBN 978-0-9790956-0-3
1. Wilson, Sylvia and Danny. 2. Dogs. 3. Dog Training. 4. Canine Behavior. 2007

PRINTED IN THE UNITED STATES OF AMERICA
5 4 3 2 1

Contents

This book is dedicated to all Bark Busters therapists around the world who work tirelessly to assist dog owners and to save dogs' lives. To those therapists in all parts of the world who work for the betterment of all dogs wherever they may be, we salute you and thank you for your dedication, passion and your belief in the Bark Busters system.

DANNY AND SYLVIA WILSON
FOUNDERS OF BARK BUSTERS HOME DOG TRAINING
WWW.BARKBUSTERS.COM

Foreword

Sylvia and Danny Wilson—both Australians and both grand master dog behavioral therapists—have spent a lifetime working with dogs and their owners. It is not only their profession but also their passion. Aussies have a unique affinity when it comes to animals, and Danny and Sylvia are no exception. As we have learned through years of working with Sylvia and Danny, many dog owners buy a dog with the intention that it will be a member of the family, but they shockingly discover that the dog has become the de facto head of the household. How does this happen?

Dogs are pack animals. A dog's instinctive behavior is to challenge the pack member above it and, in turn, to be challenged by the dog below. Within the human-dog pack, dogs behave the same way. This can lead to undesirable behaviors, such as charging the door when the doorbell rings, barking, jumping, pulling on the leash and even biting—all major reasons why millions of dogs are mistreated, abandoned or euthanized every year.

Understanding and controlling dog behavior is the mission of Bark Busters Home Dog Training, the company Sylvia and Danny founded in Australia in1989, and it is the central theme of this book. Dog behavior is a major issue in the U.S. Analysis of available statistics show that nearly two million dogs are brought to shelters each year, primarily because of behavior problems their owners believe to be permanent. The vast majority of these animals are "put to sleep," making death from behavioral problems the leading cause of

dog mortality, ahead of trauma and disease. This means a staggering number of dogs—nearly 70 percent of those given to shelters—are euthanized every year; sadly, the vast majority unnecessarily. And worst of all, it's not the dog's fault. It's a human-canine communications issue. That's why we believe dog owners will find the methods described in *Training Dogs the Aussie Way* invaluable. After all, these methods are part of the curriculum we use to train dog behavioral therapists at the Bark Busters National Training Academy in Denver, Colorado.

As you will learn from this book, dogs speak a unique language based on tones and body language that is designed to demonstrate leadership. Dogs will instinctively submit to the leader of the pack. And, for dog owners, that leadership must be communicated in a way dogs can understand. As master dog behavioral therapists who have trained thousands of dogs in Australia and the U.S., we know that dogs need clear and consistent leadership to feel safe and happy, whether within their packs or with their human families. Allowing a dog to assume a higher position within the family than his temperament is able to handle creates stress, just like a person who is promoted to a position above his or her ability. However, a dog's need for a strong leader is instinctive, and if in its mind a human companion is not up to the task, the dog will constantly challenge the human for leadership.

We've all seen this scenario: the hapless human stumbling down the sidewalk, dragged by the dominating dog. It's a classic suburban image—but it need not be that way. There is no reason for your dog to lead you on walks, cut you off on the stairs, run first through open doorways, jump on visitors, or bark every time the doorbell rings or a child walks by your house. Typically, these are behaviors of dogs who think they are in charge. The lesson for dog owners in this book is to take control by communicating leadership—and do so consistently. Bark Busters dog behavioral therapists around the world have successfully trained hundreds of thousands of dogs of every age and breed by following the methods in *Training Dogs the Aussie Way.*

Another key point: discipline and leadership are not enemies of fun. And in no way should training a dog inhibit its playfulness or spontaneity. But that doesn't mean there should be no rules for inappropriate behavior. In fact, providing your dog with consistent leadership and ground rules for behavior will make it feel more secure and relaxed and make for a more self-assured companion. Dogs must learn who is in charge in a "language" they understand. Remember, training is part of the responsibility of dog ownership, just as much as providing food and shelter—all aspects of creating a happy, secure, and stable family.

Most dog owners simply accept the disruptive or aggressive behavior of their dogs because they think it's normal or don't know how to change it. Learning about pack leadership and canine communication is incredibly interesting for dog lovers. And gaining a better understanding of the dog psyche strengthens the human-canine connection. Learning how to communicate leadership effectively with your dog in a language it understands—using voice tones and body language—is a critical step in establishing leadership and control, which can eliminate many behavioral issues. Through effective training and communications methods that demonstrate leadership, most dogs can be saved from abandonment or euthanasia, and can become the loving companions we all want.

We invite you to enjoy *Training Dogs the Aussie Way,* a compilation of Sylvia and Danny's lifetime of remarkable work. Moreover, we encourage you to put the unique, all-natural techniques into practice—and you, too, can experience the joy that a well-trained canine companion can provide. If you have questions or want to speak to a Bark Busters therapist, visit us at www.BarkBusters.com.

—Andrew Brooke & Liam Crowe,
Co-founders of Bark Busters USA

How to Use This Book

Owning a dog can be one of the most rewarding experiences in life, for both you and your pet. Unfortunately, despite the fact that most dog owners truly care about their animals, common misconceptions about their behavior result in far too many dogs being surrendered to shelters, sometimes for what are easily corrected problems. Each year, an estimated eight to twelve million companion animals enter shelters in the United States. More than half of those surrendered are dogs, and approximately sixty percent of them are euthanized.

The good news is that most dogs can be successfully trained, even those that have been abused or allowed to develop bad habits as a result of inadequate or no training. We have written this book to help current or prospective owners understand dogs better: how they think and why they act the way they do. Equipped with this fundamental knowledge, you will then learn techniques that can be used to train a dog in a matter of weeks, if not days, and to correct behavioral problems, sometimes in only a few minutes. The result will be a more positive relationship between you and your dog, as opposed to one fraught with frustration and potentially disastrous consequences.

The information and techniques shared in this book are based on more than forty years of personal experience working with dogs and observing how they relate to one another. We have developed a program that has been successfully used by Bark Busters therapists to train literally hundreds of thousands of dogs around the world and is one that nearly anyone can learn and employ. You will be surprised at how easily and quickly you can achieve results and how much more content your dog will be.

The most effective way to use this book is to read Sections One and Two in their entirety before moving on to the specific training and behavior problem-solving techniques covered in the rest of the book. Section One explains, in relatively simple terms, what it means to be a dog (its instinctive nature), how dogs communicate and learn, and why training is imperative to ensure your dog's quality of life, if not its survival. Section Two provides specifics on choosing the best dog for your lifestyle and how to properly care for your dog. In subsequent sections, you will learn the basic training techniques employed successfully by Bark Busters therapists, as well as how to correct some of the most common behavioral problems. We will also cover what to do in special circumstances, such as bringing a new baby home, and how to teach your dog (even an old one) new tricks.

But you have to do your homework first. The key is having a solid understanding of the principles behind the training program, which then can be applied to nearly any situation. There have been numerous books written on the subject of dog training, but we've found most are too complicated for those who just want to care for and enjoy their pets, not get a degree in animal behavior.

In contrast, our goal is to make dog ownership as simple and as enjoyable as possible. You already possess the most important characteristic to be a successful dog owner and trainer: a love of dogs and a desire to know more. Now all you have to do is turn the page and begin the learning process.

SECTION ONE
Understanding Your Dog

If you are struggling with a dog that disobeys or misbehaves, don't be too hard on yourself. No one is born a dog trainer. We all have to learn. The biggest challenges are the myriad misconceptions about dogs. These myths can cause us to behave in certain ways or utilize ill-advised training techniques that actually create more problems than they solve. It is our belief that there are no bad dogs, only misunderstood ones. Throughout this book, we will dispel many of those myths, while sharing our secrets to raising and owning happy, healthy, and well-behaved dogs.

MYTH #1: MY DOG THINKS THE SAME WAY I DO.
Perhaps the most common and detrimental misconception about dogs is that they think like humans and therefore should act accordingly. To effectively train a dog, you must first understand its basic nature, that of a pack animal.

THE NATURE OF THE PACK

In the wild, dogs have always lived in packs. Although domesticated for thousands of years, dogs still live by the same rules and exhibit many of the same behavioral patterns as their wild ancestors. They instinctively know that living with others, under the leadership of the most dominant member of the pack, enhances not only their chances for survival but also that of future generations. In nature, the leader of the pack would hunt and eat first, followed by the next most dominant member and so on. In most cases, the pack leader would be the only male or female to mate. All of these factors work to ensure that the genes and attributes of the leader are passed on to the pack's offspring.

The pack leader is determined by a number of observable characteristics, including physical strength, consistency of behavior, and body language. Rarely would a pack leader rule for life. As a leader ages, it may begin to exhibit a less dominant posture and more inconsistent behavior. For example, it might back away from confrontation one day, only to face the next one head on. This behavior sends a message to other members of the pack, especially younger dogs that have already successfully demonstrated their dominance over their contemporaries during play, that there is an opportunity to become the top, or alpha, dog.

In simple terms, pack animals want to live with others and are content with a leader who is strong, consistent, and fair. As long as a dog owner exhibits those same characteristics, he or she will be accepted as the dog's leader, with the other humans and animals living in the home making up the rest of the pack.

CASE STUDY

A four-year-old German shepherd, Max, consistently demonstrated good behavior toward a family who clearly loved him. Daniel, the family's fourteen-year-old son, was Max's constant companion. Unlike his parents,

Daniel was reluctant to correct Max for fear the dog would not like him anymore. One day, when Daniel went to take Max for his walk, Max inexplicably attacked Daniel as the boy reached for a stick the dog had been chewing. The resulting injury required five stitches. Fearing they would have to put Max down, Daniel's father called Bark Busters for help.

We explained to the family that, as a pack animal, a dog follows certain instincts: it will act like the boss toward any member of the pack it can dominate, in this case, Daniel. By failing to show dominance over Max, Daniel had not earned the dog's respect. Max did not intend to injure Daniel, only correct him for taking the stick. We recommended training as a way for Max to learn to respect and obey Daniel.

MYTH #2: MY DOG DISOBEYS BECAUSE IT IS STUPID OR VINDICTIVE.

When we are called in to address behavioral problems in dogs, we often hear their owners say things like, "My dog doesn't obey because it's stupid" or "It destroys things out of spite." There are a multitude of reasons why dogs misbehave, but lack of intelligence and spite are not among them. Knowing what the real reasons are requires an understanding of how dogs think and learn.

When a dog disobeys, it is usually for one of three reasons: 1) it does not understand what you want, 2) it does not consider you its leader, or 3) it is suffering from some kind of stress or fear. For example, as social animals, some dogs will act inappropriately when they are left alone or associate something in the environment with a prior bad experience. Throughout this book, we will cover the specific reasons why dogs misbehave and how to address them. By understanding the true nature of dogs, you will be better prepared to diagnose problems yourself and employ the training techniques outlined in this book to correct them.

MYTH #3: MY DOG UNDERSTANDS EVERYTHING I SAY.

Many would-be dog trainers make the mistake of trying to communicate with their dogs in the same way they would with another person. To believe your dog fully understands human-based communication is as absurd as thinking you know everything your dog is saying when it barks. If you consider your dog a member of the family, it's natural to want to include it in your conversations. But speaking in full sentences or paragraphs will only confuse your dog. It will look at you in bewilderment, turning its head from side to side in a sincere but futile effort to understand.

Dogs have a very distinct way of communicating, limited primarily to barking, growling, and other guttural sounds that are reinforced and usually superseded by body language. More dominant dogs will use both sound and body language to exert their authority and educate other members of the pack. From a very early age, a puppy learns that if it does not immediately respond to the growl of its mother or another more dominant pack member, it will be corrected with a nip or some other, harsher corrective action.

Even more than sound, dogs rely heavily on body language to communicate what's on their minds. If they are feeling frightened and weak, they will lower their height. If they are feeling confident and strong, they will stand tall.

The Bark Busters training technique uses the same method of communication as dogs. By using a language that dogs instinctively understand, you can shorten the time it takes to train your dog. Liken it to the difference between teaching someone in his or her native tongue, as compared to a foreign language. Eventually, you can teach a dog to relate some simple words with the desired response, but that can take months to accomplish. That's why Bark Busters therapists spend the bulk of their time teaching dog owners how to communicate with their pets. Once the owners understand the theory and training techniques, their dogs can be trained in a matter of hours, if not minutes.

To maximize the effectiveness of this approach, you need to copy your dog's communication style as closely as possible. When correcting or disciplining your dog, do so in exactly the same way another dog would express its disapproval, with a growl and a posture that depicts dominance.

USING THE CORRECTIVE WORD "BAH"

At Bark Busters, we substitute the word "BAH" [bɐh] for the growl. BAH is not a magic word on its own. Spoken in a normal tone or without the correct body language, it will probably be ignored by a dog. But if you say it in a deep, guttural tone at exactly the same time the dog is doing something you want it to stop, you will almost always get the desired response.

WHY NOT "NO"?

Some question why we suggest using the word "BAH" rather than the word "NO" to let a dog know it is doing something wrong. The reason is simple: NO is not a word a dog will naturally comprehend. Teaching a dog that NO means "Stop what you are doing" takes time, sometimes months, whereas the dog will understand the sound of a growl instantly. The rounded sound of the word NO also makes it extremely difficult to say in the same manner as a growl. The only time dogs make a sound similar to NO is when they are howling.

Once you have chosen your corrective word, whether it is BAH or something comparable, use only that word and that word alone to express disapproval. Including BAH as part of a longer statement will only confuse your dog. Consistency in your approach will help you establish authority and enable your dog to learn as quickly as possible.

CASE STUDY

One of our more memorable experiences was with a little Yorkshire terrier that we had been asked to train for the stage play "Gypsy." We found a likely stray at the local pound and named him Chowsie after the doggy character in the play.

Chowsie had no previous training and would snap at anyone who tried to pick him up. We conditioned him first with the BAH correction and then accustomed him to being carried everywhere by reassuring him with praise. The more pressing problem, however, was his reluctance to come when called, an awkward trait for a budding actor. This time, we used both the BAH technique and a Bark Busters training pillow. (See Section Three for more on the training pillow.) Whenever he tried to run away, we would toss the training pillow near his feet. The presence of the pillow would startle him and cause him to stop (much like a correction he would receive from another dog). Then we could praise him for coming back to us.

After a successful training session that lasted only half an hour, it was time for Chowsie's first rehearsal. We confidently drove Chowsie to the rehearsal hall, unaware that an assistant had loosened his collar. As we got out of our vehicle, Chowsie slipped out of his collar and darted down the busy street. We began to race after him, calling his name, when we quickly realized our error. We stopped in our tracks and growled BAH! The little dog immediately turned and ran back to us. Thanks to the fast-acting nature of the Bark Busters training method, we were able to save Chowsie's life (and our reputations). Chowsie completed fourteen performances in the play and was a huge success.

THE CORRECT VOCAL TONE

A common mistake made by dog owners is using the wrong vocal tone when attempting to communicate with their animals. A harsh voice can be interpreted as a growl by a dog, while a high-pitched voice sounds the same as that used by dogs, and particularly puppies, when they are excited. If you want your dog to come to you, your voice needs to sound inviting by using a high-pitched "Good boy (or girl)," followed by COME! A dog will be less likely to come if you are yelling at it. Other commands, such as SIT, STAY, or DROP, should be delivered in a normal speaking voice. We will cover commands in more detail in Section Three.

Correct Vocal Tone	Purpose	Example
Low growl	Correcting a dog's misbehavior	BAH
High-pitched	Praising Asking your dog to come	Good Dog COME
Normal speaking voice	Commands	SIT, STAY, DROP

CASE STUDY

Bark Busters was called in to work with the new owners of a lively Brittany spaniel. On the afternoon we visited, as soon as the door opened, the Brittany took the opportunity to run through our legs, racing across the street into a large park. The panicked owners began to chase the dog, yelling for it to come back. Sensing a game, the dog looked over its shoulder and continued running. I called for the owners to stop, but they shouted, "He'll be gone if we don't chase him." I asked his name, knelt down, and called in a sing-song voice, "Here, Casey. Come, boy. Good boy, Casey. Come on." I patted my thighs as I coaxed the dog to my side. The owners were amazed.

What had failed in the owners' approach? It was a combination of commonly made errors. First, they called the dog's name without providing a command. A dog's name should be used only to get its attention; with no attached command, the dog does not know what is expected. Second, they chased the dog. That just makes a dog think you have joined in the game. Third, their posture and harsh voice tones were threatening to the dog. By crouching or kneeling (even lying down if necessary) and speaking in an inviting voice, you can entice your dog to come to you.

MATCHING BODY LANGUAGE

If your dog ignores you when you growl BAH in the correct vocal tone, you may be using the wrong body language. It may not recognize your authority if you are sitting in a chair or another position viewed as inferior by your dog. At a lower height, you are in a less dominant position than the dog; in other words, while you might sound dominant, your body is portraying submission. In such a case, your dog might even interpret your use of the word BAH as fear instead of dominance.

There are also times when you can communicate better with your dog by actually lowering your stance. For example, if you are calling a runaway puppy, stop in your tracks, crouch down, and call your puppy in a soft, melodic voice. Then, as your puppy approaches, stand up. When it arrives (but not sooner) praise it and give it a pat. If it stops short of coming to you, stand up and give it a corrective BAH sound. Do not pat a puppy that rolls over on its back. Instead, back away, crouch down, and call it to you.

Body language can also be misinterpreted. If a dog jumps up on you and you respond by pushing it down with both hands, the dog may think you want to play, in much the same way it would play with other dogs. Instead of the dog staying down (as you would prefer), it jumps up again. Let the games begin! If you use a harsh tone to correct the dog, it can become even more confused. Now, it will likely jump up in an attempt to play and then dart away to avoid the scolding.

We will provide guidelines on proper body language for the specific training techniques later in this book.

MYTH #3: DISCIPLINING A DOG IS CRUEL.

Just as there are ongoing debates about whether you should discipline a child, some consider disciplining dogs to be cruel. Once, while helping an owner teach her dog how to walk on its lead, a woman passed us on the street and indignantly said, "It's a dog, not a robot." She clearly felt that what we were doing, which included the use of discipline as a training tool, to be either unnecessary or inappropriate.

On the contrary, we firmly believe that dogs want and need to be trained. It's a matter of survival. Without adequate training, a dog can get in trouble, which could lead to its destruction. At the very least, the dog could end up being confined, and a lack of social interaction can be the cruelest punishment for a pack animal. In the wild, a dog would be educated and disciplined first by its mother and throughout its life by more dominant pack members. They would teach it how to hunt and to play, everything it needed to survive. As dog owners, one of our responsibilities is to fill the role of educator. We must teach our dogs how to survive in society.

To develop normally, both puppies and children need to know the rules regarding what is acceptable and what is not. Imagine a two-year-old child who kicks others. If the child's parents took no disciplinary action, their silence would send a message to the child that his or her behavior is acceptable.

It is the same for dogs. They will only do what their instincts tell them, unless they are trained to do otherwise. As a result, they can act in ways we might view as disobedient. Unfortunately, far too many animals are destroyed each year because their owners fail to recognize that their dogs need to be taught how to behave in order not to become nuisances or perceived as threats by others.

CASE STUDY

Clancy was a two-year-old rogue Rottweiler. His owners exercised no control over their dog and allowed him to run free. His last day of freedom went something like this:

Clancy was lured by the scent of freshly baked cream cakes coming from a delivery van parked outside a bakery. In the driver's absence, Clancy clambered into the van to investigate the intriguing aroma. When the driver returned, he screamed at the sight of the Rottweiler's massive jaw dripping with cream. Clancy leapt from the truck, knocking down the driver and horrifying onlookers who assumed the driver had been attacked. Their shouts further panicked the dog, who ran into the street. An oncoming car veered to avoid the dog and crashed into the baker's van. The baker rang the police to report a savage dog on the loose.

Clancy, meanwhile, returned home, none the worse for his experience and still sporting cream on his jaws. When the police arrived, Clancy was playing in his backyard peacefully. The escapade cost Clancy's owners thousands of dollars in damages and Clancy his freedom. He was never allowed out of his yard again.

CASE STUDY

Candy, a 15-month-old bichon frise, was inordinately spoiled by her owner. The dog's wardrobe was impressive: seven coats with matching leads. She slept on a water bed, enjoyed her own stereo, and consumed a specially controlled diet at her own table and chair. Still, Candy was not a happy dog. Unprovoked, she had attacked and bit her owner several times for no apparent reason, once so severely her owner had to be hospitalized.

Candy's owner was baffled; she believed that pampering her dog would make Candy love her in return. But a dog's love is based on respect, not coddling. We advised the owner that Candy would have to receive corrective therapy on a daily basis, a method called conditioning (and described in Section Three). Candy could still have her special treats, but she must also have rules. Happily, once Candy's owner won her respect, the dog stopped snapping. Our adage is: Treat a dog like a human and it will treat you like a dog.

The concern about disciplining dogs may stem from confusion over what we mean by the term "discipline." It does not mean the same thing as "punishment." In fact, two of Bark Busters' most important tenets are never train your dog in anger and never use physical force. This is one of the problems we see with the popular "alpha rolling" training method. This technique employs what is known as the alpha roll ("alpha" referring to the "number one" or "top" dog) as a means for an owner to assert his or her dominance over a puppy. The owner is instructed to roll the puppy over on its back, pin it to the ground, and hold it there for a short period until the dog stops struggling. To the untrained eye, dominant dogs in a pack appear to utilize a similar method to discipline their subordinates, but there are subtle differences. First, the dog rolls over by itself, out of respect for the more dominant animal. Second, the dog that is dishing out the discipline does not use its paws (comparable to the hands of an owner). Instead, it uses its mouth to snap and growl in order to get the offending dog to listen. Its mouth does not come in contact with the dog, nor is it used to harm or maim the less dominant animal.

CASE STUDY

The owner of Caesar, a seven-month-old German shepherd puppy, was very distressed about his dog's behavior. Caesar had ferociously attacked his owners without apparent provocation. Most of the dog experts he had consulted advocated euthanasia, but the owner wanted to explore other options.

He explained to us that the dog training classes he was taking had taught him to alpha roll his dog. The method had appeared to work when Caesar was a small puppy, but as the dog grew, it became increasingly difficult to get the dog to submit to rolling over.

Around this time, another problem arose: Caesar had begun to bark in the back of his owner's van. The trainers told him to try the alpha rolling technique again. He followed their instructions. When the dog barked, the owner would stop the car, jump into the back of his van, and wrestle his dog to the ground.

He did this several times until he was driving one day and a young boy suddenly rode his bike in front of the van. The owner slammed on the brakes, and Caesar suddenly attacked him from behind.

Now, why would a dog that had never bitten anyone suddenly attack its owner?

We believe the dog associated the slamming of brakes with the impending punishment and decided to unleash a sneak attack while his owner was not looking.

Any use of physical force can stimulate the "flight or fight" response in a dog. The flight response can be triggered by the fear a dog may feel when it is dragged back to the scene of the crime and punished, alpha-rolled or smacked for not obeying. However, a dog that is restrained by a collar or picked up may feel like it has no other option but to fight. It learns quickly that if its owner grabs it, the fastest way to get free is to bite its owner.

Dogs learn to outsmart owners who use physical force. The best way to correct your dog's mistakes is by using the correct body language coupled with the growled word BAH. If your dog continues to ignore you, you can escalate the degree of discipline, as outlined in the Sliding Scale of Correction discussed in Section Three.

CASE STUDY

We were called by a man who had just purchased a six-week-old Rottweiler pup named Rover and was having problems getting the dog to come to him. In our experience, even the most timid pup will approach its new owner. But it had been a week, and the man said the dog avoided him from day one.

When we saw Rover, the dog happily approached us, but not to the point we could reach him. However, if we crouched down and held out our hands, the pup would allow us to scratch his chin, but not the top of his head.

After questioning the owner, we learned that Rover had relieved himself on the living room floor the day he was brought home. The owner misguidedly grabbed the pup by the scruff of his neck, rubbed the dog's nose in his droppings, and unceremoniously booted him outside. From that day on, the pup would not let anyone close enough to do this again.

Rover was fully rehabilitated with therapy involving crouching and gentle reconditioning to teach him that the hand that had hurt him before would not hurt him again. The owner could have avoided the problem by observing the golden rule: Never use your hands in anger when dealing with your dog.

Using the correct form of discipline to teach your dog what is wrong is one of the best ways to care for and love your pet. Even more importantly, use praise to let your dog know when it has done something right.

Even some who understand the need to educate and train their dogs question the use of discipline. In keeping with some modern-day child psychology theories, they contend that you should only use positive reinforcement to teach a dog. Praise given in a manner that lets a dog know immediately when it has done something "right" is critical to effective training, but it is only half of the puzzle; it offers no solution for stopping negative behavior. The idea behind positive reinforcement is that the puppy will choose to be good rather than bad because it receives praise when it is good. But that assumes dogs, like humans, have the capacity to reason and to distinguish between right and wrong.

MYTH #4: MY DOG KNOWS IT HAS DONE SOMETHING WRONG.

We hear this statement from countless dog owners. As much as we may want to believe our dogs think like us, they can't. It's a matter of simple biology.

Human brains are made up of three separate sections, giving us the capacity for subconscious thought, intelligence, and reasoning. Dogs, on the other hand, have only two sections to their brain, leaving them without the ability to reason. That's why, for example, some dogs cannot figure out that they are stronger than humans.

Since they are unable to distinguish between right and wrong, dogs cannot feel guilty about misbehaving. Some owners contend that they have come home to find their dogs acting guilty when they have done something wrong. Chances are their dogs are really exhibiting fear and submission, probably because they associate their owners' return or the presence of something, such as trash on the floor, with being scolded, not with anything they have done. What we interpret as guilt is actually just plain fear that a bad experience will be repeated.

CASE STUDY

Shandy was a 12-month-old golden retriever with an annoying habit of pulling wash off the line and trampling it in the mud. No matter how many times his owners had slapped him after discovering the mess, the dog continued the bad behavior.

Hitting a dog after the fact only frightens and confuses it. A dog cannot associate the punishment with the crime when the two do not occur at the same time. Shandy did not know the laundry was out of bounds, and his owners' aggressive behavior did not convey the message. Our solution was to get the laundry to issue the correction. We instructed the owners to soak some foam rubber in Bitter Apple® and then to sew the foam rubber into the hems of some old clothes. When Shandy pulled at the specially treated clothes on the line, he received an unpleasant surprise at the time of the offense. Shandy now leaves the washing alone and instead plays with some more appropriate play things provided by his owners. (See Section Two for recommendations on dog toys.)

LEARNING BY ASSOCIATION

Association and experience are the only factors other than instinct that directly impact how dogs behave. The training techniques in this book teach dogs to associate bad behavior with a bad experience, such as a voice correction, and good behavior with a good experience, such as being praised.

We cannot explain to a dog, as we would a young child, not to touch a hot stove. The only way for the dog to really learn that lesson is to touch the stove by accident. If that happens, you can be sure the dog will not touch it again, even if the stove is turned off.

Unfortunately, some bad experiences, if traumatic enough, can create phobias that prevent dogs from doing things that are necessary. For example, if the dog remembers experiencing pain at the veterinarian, it may strongly resist going again.

CASE STUDY

Some years ago, we were training a boxer that would jump and dance around at the end of the lead whenever we tried to walk it past a certain paddock. After a few days' training, we were able to get the dog to walk calmly past the area. We later learned that the dog had been stung by bees in that same paddock. Even though it had subsequently walked safely past the paddock many times, the experience with the bees had made a lasting impression that only several days of intensive training could erase.

During training, a dog may also ignore your command if you are wearing something it associates with another experience. For example, if you tend to wear a particular scarf every time you go out to feed your dog, it could become excited whenever it sees you wearing the scarf, associating it with meal time.

Myth #5: You can't teach an old dog new tricks.

The good news is that dogs are continuous learners, and you can help a dog overcome its fears by replacing the bad experience with a good one. We will discuss how to accomplish that in Section Four.

It's important to recognize that your dog may interpret an experience differently than you would. For example, a lot of dogs like to chase cars. While we might not see the point, the dog considers it a victory every time a car it chases drives away. From the dog's point of view, it was able to successfully correct the car by barking and then chasing it until it ran away (drove off). Even dogs that have been hit by cars will continue to chase them. To a dominant dog, the car did not have the authority to hit it. We will cover how to cure a dog's car chasing habit in Section Four.

Basically, a dog's brain is like a computer: it can store things and then retrieve them when triggered. Just what is stored and then recalled by a dog's brain is often dictated by how dogs literally perceive the world around them, which is different than how humans perceive it.

We mentioned earlier that dogs have very good memories that can be triggered by the sight of something familiar or more often by scent because dogs have a much better sense of smell than vision. Humans remember each other by seeing and recalling physical features; dogs, on the other hand, can identify us by the way we walk, the sound of our voice, and our individual scent. When a dog smells or sees something familiar, it will remember exactly what happened the last time. That's why a dog can meet you once and months later remember exactly who you are based on your scent and whether it was a good or a bad experience.

How a Dog Senses the World

Smell

Smell is the most dramatic sensory difference between humans and dogs. A dog can track a person through the woods by a scent that is days old, an ability developed in wild dogs that had to hunt for prey in order to survive. But dogs have their limitations. They cannot effectively distinguish scents from a distance unless the breeze is blowing in their direction. Instead, they must come close to a person to pick up his or her scent or put their noses firmly to the ground to track a scent. They will also lift their noses high in the air to try to pinpoint a smell on currents of air.

Taste

A dog's sense of smell is closely linked to taste. A dog is so scent sensitive it is usually the smell, not the taste, that will cause a dog to reject its food before it even enters its mouth. In contrast, humans have five times as many taste buds as dogs and tend to try something before deciding if they like it or not.

Vision

The dog's eye lacks certain components found in the human eye. As such, dogs probably see the world in shades of black, white, and grey and have much better night vision than humans. Generally speaking, a dog has more difficulty seeing things that are static but will see and respond quickly to something that is moving, another valuable attribute for dogs that had to hunt to survive.

Vision also varies by breed. Due to the positioning of their eyes, short-nosed dogs have better stereoscopic sight than longer-nosed breeds. In other words, they can see things in the distance with more depth perception. Many toy breeds have difficulty seeing far away.

When you are standing or walking with your dog, remember its horizon is lower than yours because its head is lower. As a result, you will see many things before your dog does. When walking, a dog will rarely look up unless something, such as a noise, catches its attention.

Hearing

Hearing is acutely developed in dogs, giving them an extraordinary ability to not only notice sounds but also identify what they are. Because they hear so well, there is no need to yell when training your dog, although you may need to raise your voice initially to get its attention. There are also training aids that serve the same purpose, which will be covered in more detail in Section Three. Once the dog is focused on you, it will usually respond to a lower growl tone much more than a yell. More importantly, never yell out of anger when disciplining a dog.

THE RIGHT WAY TO DISCIPLINE

We've already established that disciplining a dog is both appropriate and necessary. But there is a right and a wrong way to discipline. Since your dog cannot reason, it can never deliberately be naughty; a dog's behavior is always determined by either instinct or experience. Therefore, there is never a legitimate reason to get angry with your dog, since it only does what comes naturally or what it has learned through association.

Physical force is also both inappropriate and counterproductive. This includes using your hands when correcting your dog. Because dogs don't have hands themselves, they find any form of discipline by humans that involves hands to be both provocative and threatening. You should never bully, smack, or grab your dog. A dog that is regularly grabbed or hit may bite its owner in order to stop being punished.

For this reason, use your hands as little as possible when training your dog, and when you do, use them only for gentle manipulation or patting. Your dog must always associate your hands with gentleness and pleasure. We will discuss proper use of hands for training more in Sections Three and Four.

Another common but detrimental disciplinary method involves the use of a rolled-up newspaper. Although we have heard experts claim that it does not hurt the dog, we disagree. We would suggest to those experts that they try hitting themselves, or better yet, have someone else hit them with a rolled-up newspaper. But what if they are right and it doesn't hurt the dog? Then we would ask, what is the purpose? None, in our opinion. It will only make a dog more aggressive or more confused.

CASE STUDY

Bonnie, a twelve-month-old English bull terrier, belonged to John, a sea-going captain, and his wife, Angie. Whenever John went to sea, Bonnie would attack Angie if she tried to scold her. The attacks escalated in violence to the point where Captain John feared leaving his wife alone with the dog.

When Bark Busters therapists visited the home, the dog appeared affectionate and without any psychological problems. We asked Angie to demonstrate what she would do to prompt an attack. Angie stood over the dog in a menacing posture, pointed at the door, and yelled "Outside" in an aggressive tone. Immediately, the dog began growling and snapping at her owner. Bonnie's behavior was threatening, and we stopped the demonstration.

We asked Angie if she ever hit the dog with her hands or an object. Angie confirmed our suspicions. When Bonnie was a puppy, Angie had struck the dog with a rolled-up newspaper. She stopped the practice when the dog became aggressive. The newspaper combined with Angie's threatening posture and harsh tone had taught the dog to associate physical punishment with the command "Outside," provoking an attack. On the other hand, when Captain John was home, he disciplined the dog in a far less threatening manner.

We carefully conditioned Bonnie to the BAH correction command and cautioned Angie to give commands in a normal, rather than harsh, speaking voice, and to use her hands only to praise the dog. A loving relationship soon was established between Angie and Bonnie.

CASE STUDY

Chantel was an eighteen-month-old standard poodle who was left alone when her owners were at work. Her long hours of solitude created a lot of stress, evidenced by the wreckage her owners faced each day when they returned home. Chantel chewed her way through most of the wooden garden furniture and their veranda. Out of frustration, the owners would point out the damage to Chantel and attempt to discipline her with a rolled-up newspaper. Their failure to correct the behavior made them consider getting rid of her.

When Bark Busters visited the home, Chantel was agitated and nervous, darting about the yard. The owners pointed to the chewed garden furniture and asked, "Who did this?" Chantel cringed, her ears pinned back. The owners were convinced this behavior meant Chantel knew she'd done something wrong.

We explained that Chantel was only responding to their anger, not to the damaged furniture. We instructed the owners to condition Chantel to the BAH word as a correction. We then suggested they pretend to leave Chantel alone, only to sneak back and catch and correct her in the act of chewing. The surprise caused by their reappearance would make Chantel think they might always be around, thereby reducing her anxiety. As reinforcement, we also suggested they paint their furniture with Bitter Apple® or another safe doggy repellent. Chantel's behavior was corrected within a week.

The biggest problem with these and other forms of discipline that employ punishment is that they do not teach your dog why you are displeased or what you want the dog to do differently.

THE RIGHT TIME TO DISCIPLINE/PRAISE

Because dogs learn by association, they will only comprehend your message if it is delivered in a timely manner. A correction must be issued at the precise moment that the dog is either contemplating or actually doing something wrong, not after the fact. This means that all corrections must be delivered at exactly the right time. Dragging a dog back to the "scene of the crime" to punish it will only make your dog fearful of you and your hands.

You can determine if a dog is considering doing something inappropriate even before it misbehaves by watching its focus. It will first look at the object or situation before acting. For example, if you wanted to stop a child from taking something, the best time to stop him would be just as he indicates his intention to reach for the object.

Sometimes it might be difficult to catch your dog in the act. In those cases, you can create situations that will cause a dog to misbehave and then correct it in a timely manner. This technique, known as "scene setting," will be discussed in more detail in Section Three.

CASE STUDY

Harry, a fifteen-month-old cocker spaniel, refused to stay in the laundry room at night where he was supposed to sleep. He scratched at the door and barked, disturbing the owner. We asked the owner if he had caught Harry in the act. "Oh, yes, several times," was the response. The owner explained that when he heard the dog barking, he would get out of bed, walk to the laundry, open the door and swat the dog with a rolled-up newspaper. We explained that this was not catching the dog in the act. Instead, the door was now open, and the dog was simply looking at its owner.

To correct this behavior at the proper time, we suggested the owner growl BAH and throw a Bark Busters training pillow at the closed door while the dog is barking and scratching. (We will discuss the training pillow in more detail in Section Three.) Harry responded after only a few well-timed corrections were made while he was barking; both dog and owner were able to sleep through the night undisturbed.

We've spent considerable time discussing the importance of discipline and how to appropriately correct your dog, and we will cover more specifics in Section Three. Remember, knowing how to correct your dog is designed to give you the opportunity to praise your dog. When your dog does what you want, let it know you are pleased with its behavior. Praise your dog in a soft, melodic voice using the same words every time, such as "Good boy" or "Good girl." It's important that your dog learns these are words of praise because it may not always be close enough for you to reach out and pat it. Of course, when your dog is near, pat it gently and warmly.

Understanding your dog's nature and how it learns is necessary to train it effectively and to ensure its safety and well-being. In Section Two, you will learn how to select the best dog for your personality and lifestyle and how to raise it to be a healthy and happy animal.

SECTION TWO
Raising a Well-Behaved Dog

We learned in Section One that two things primarily influence a dog's behavior: instinct and experience. However, a dog's breed and temperament, combined with your lifestyle and personality, all play an important role in determining what kind of dog is best for you and how easy it will be to train.

Owning a dog is a decision to be considered carefully. As we have discussed, it is your responsibility to ensure that your dog can adjust well and live safely in human society. Before adopting a dog, ask yourself these questions:

- Is your house and yard set up to properly keep a dog?
- Can you devote the time necessary to care for and train a dog?
- Will you be around enough to provide the kind of companionship a pack animal needs?
- Will your dog need to get along with other people (including children) or animals, or do you want a pet that is more protective of you and your belongings?

- Have you researched everything you need to know about dogs and their needs?

Beyond lifestyle considerations, it is important to choose an animal that fits your personality. For instance, a frail, docile person could find a large-breed dog difficult to control, especially one that is boisterous or hyperactive. Correspondingly, a timid little dog may not be a suitable match for a person with a strong will.

In this section, we will discuss how to select the right dog for you, the characteristics of the various breeds, and the role temperament plays in training. We will also cover basic puppy and dog care, including medical needs, diet and nutrition, and how to create a safe environment, among others.

SELECTING THE RIGHT DOG FOR YOU

If you are a prospective dog owner or are considering getting another dog, the first question to ask is: Do you want a puppy or an older pet? There are certain advantages to adopting a puppy: you will be able to choose an animal with the best temperament for you and ensure it gets a proper education before behavioral problems or bad habits develop. But there are added responsibilities, too. During the first few months, a puppy generally requires more of your time than an older dog does. Puppies should not be left alone for extended periods of time. They need to be fed several times a day, constantly protected, and handled with care. Owners must fill the void created when they take a dog away from its mother and littermates. If you do not have the time required for a young puppy, it might be better to get a fully grown dog that has already gone through this initial adjustment period.

The primary benefit of adopting an older dog is that the puppy stage is over. Usually an older dog will be housebroken and no longer apt to chew anything and everything within reach. Training can begin immediately, but remember, as a newcomer to your family, even older dogs require a lot of attention and understanding. Before adopting an older dog, try to discover as much about its background as possible, including details of its diet. If adopting a dog from another home, ask for a favorite item, such as a toy, that the dog can take with it. If you expect it to serve as a guard dog, keep in mind that it will take approximately two weeks before the dog starts to consider your home its territory and begin protecting it.

ONE PUPPY OR TWO?

We are often asked whether two puppies should be adopted or purchased at the same time, and our answer is always the same: "Only if you genuinely want two dogs." Otherwise, you will have twice the work, and two pups are also not necessarily going to be more content than one. Some pups just want their mother; even their littermates cannot replace that need.

One disadvantage of having two pups is that as they grow, they may have serious fights to establish pack leadership. This is less dramatic if the two pups are male and female because the male normally will back down and allow the female to rule. Nevertheless, we do get calls where this has not been the case, especially if the female is overly domineering and the male becomes fearful. This personality combination can lead to fights. There are cases in which a male dog is also very dominant and refuses to back down, regardless of how dominant the other dog is and whether or not it is female. Fortunately, this is not common.

Two puppies of the same sex are a worse combination, and even neutering may not alleviate the squabbling. If you do decide to buy two puppies from the same litter, choose a male and female provided you intend to have them both neutered. (See the Benefits of Neutering and Spaying later in this section.) It is not a good idea to select a small-breed puppy and a large-breed puppy. If they start squabbling, the size difference could present difficulties.

Another option would be to get a dog and a kitten at the same time. They make great mates at this age and will likely remain good friends for life. The kitten may even house-train the puppy automatically. In most cases the puppy will follow the good toilet habits of the kitten and use the litter tray.

CHOOSING THE BEST BREED TO MATCH YOUR PERSONALITY

Almost all puppies are adorable and loving. As a result, statistics show that the vast majority of decisions to adopt a puppy are made on impulse. Unfortunately, such quick decision-making means many people have not taken the time to consider what kind of dog the puppy will grow up to be. Before adopting a puppy or even a full-grown dog, investigate the breed that best suits your needs. For what purpose was the breed originally bred? For example, those that were bred to be guard dogs will be less friendly toward strangers, while dogs bred for fighting may be good with other people but not other animals.

We have listed some of the most popular dog breeds below and, based on our experience with thousands of dogs worldwide, how their personalities and characteristics might match the requirements of different types of owners. We mention some of the potential problems associated with certain breeds, but don't let that completely deter you from a breed you would otherwise like to own. Most problems can be avoided or cured utilizing the training techniques and problem-solving skills outlined in Sections Three and Four.

For more information on choosing the best breed for you, you can also visit www.BarkBusters.com.

Dogs with Soft, Even Temperaments

Beagle
The most amiable of the hound group, beagles have a soft and cuddly nature that makes them great lap dogs. Their relentless pursuit of a scent can be annoying to some owners, but this can be addressed by training them at a young age to come when called.

Labrador Retriever
One of the world's most popular breeds, the Labrador has an even temperament which has historically made it a great family dog, as well as suitable for a guide dog or for use in therapy. Bred mainly to fetch birds for hunters and return them whole and intact, Labradors are very easily trained and can be taught to fetch domestic items, such as newspapers and slippers. Although they are lovable and energetic, they are chronic chewers and can be quite destructive during their first two years. Also, don't be surprised if you find your Labrador sitting near the table begging for food scraps. This breed is prone to obesity, and its diet must be watched carefully.

Unfortunately, in recent years, we have seen more hyperactive characteristics in Labradors, which can make them difficult to train. Be very selective and steer away from hyperactive puppies.

Golden Retriever
Often mistaken for a long-coated Labrador, the golden retriever shares many of the same characteristics with the Labrador but has a softer temperament and less exuberant nature.

Old English Sheepdog
This breed was made famous by Walt Disney movies and tends to attract a lot of attention in public. Old English sheepdogs have a soft, amiable temperament

and the capacity to romp and play all day long, making them great family dogs. Their lack of concentration, however, can make training more difficult than with other breeds. Although training should be attempted early, best results are achieved when the dog is two to four years of age.

Shetland Sheepdog

This is one of the less demanding and more soft-natured breeds, although some animals that have been spoiled by their owners may appear to be dominant when they are not. Shetlands can be prone to barking, due to their breeding as sheepdogs and the need to bark to move the herd. Shetland sheepdogs are very clean and fastidious dogs, although their coats require considerable care and attention. Liking nothing more than to spend hours curled up with their owners, these loving dogs have a very docile temperament that makes them perfect for the elderly and families with children.

Siberian Husky

Huskies are generally very lovable dogs. Bred as sled dogs, Siberian huskies have to be taught from an early age not to pull while on the lead. If you are looking for a sled dog, we recommend a husky over the more strong-willed malamute. Huskies have a tendency to roam but are very trainable. Howling can also be a bothersome behavioral characteristic.

Whippet

Like the greyhound, this breed loves chasing anything that moves. With just some basic training, a whippet can be easily controlled and is well suited for a soft-natured person, as long as the dog gets plenty of exercise.

Dogs that Require More Discipline

Afghan Hound

The elegant stride of these dogs when they run (which they love to do) is beautiful to behold, but it can be difficult to get them to stop or come when called. These dogs require lots of exercise, but their energy and loyal, loving natures make them wonderful family pets. It is only the combination of their size and exuberance that makes them harder to control than some other breeds.

Boxer

The strong physique of a boxer matches its very exuberant personality. Boxers are great for people with lots of energy. They are easy to train, but they are not suited for soft-natured owners because they require discipline. They possess a very amiable nature and make loyal and loving pets for families with children. On the negative side, slobbering can be a problem.

Bull Terrier

Bull terriers are lovable, trustworthy dogs when it comes to people, but they tend to act unsociably around other animals. This is understandable given that they were bred originally to control cattle and later as fighting animals. They are quite trainable, despite the fact that some mistake their stubbornness for lack of intelligence. Tough dogs that play hard, they are not suited for timid owners. Since they are not active dogs, don't be surprised if they just drop wherever they are and refuse to move when they run out of energy. Prone to allergies, bull terriers should be fed a preservative-free diet.

English Cocker Spaniel

Careful breeding over the years has succeeded in eliminating many undesirable traits from this very vivacious breed, but they are still prone to temperament swings when they are not happy. These energetic dogs often act like a wound-up spring. Without discipline to fully control them, they can become overexcited and erratic. Barking can also be a problem if not curbed early.

Dachshund

Bred to catch rats in their native Germany, this tenacious breed is prone to plenty of barking, and their instinctive drive to dig can cause real problems. Despite their diminutive size, they require discipline.

Dalmatian

Dalmatians have an even temperament that makes them good guard dogs. This is a very energetic breed that needs room to move, as well as discipline to overcome an "I'll get to it when I'm ready" approach to life.

Doberman Pinscher

Originally bred as guard dogs from the pinschers and Rottweilers, these dogs have two main downsides: a tendency not to come when called and a habit of chewing through their leads when tied up. Although they are often depicted in the media as ferocious animals, Doberman pinschers are actually both loving and dependable. Like all dogs, they should be obedience trained from an early age.

German Shepherd

These are remarkably adaptable dogs, both loyal and trustworthy, if trained from an early age. Normally very intelligent, their negative characteristics are usually excessive aggression toward strangers, fence jumping, and hole digging. German shepherds not only make good guard dogs but also great pets, if you are selective in terms of temperament and avoid timid, frightened types.

Great Dane

Great Danes may be the tallest dogs in the world, but they are also among the most docile. Their sheer size means they need to be strictly controlled and trained from an early age. They can be lots of fun but are potentially too overbearing for small children.

Miniature Schnauzer

Don't let their cute looks deceive you. Like most German breeds, these compact dogs need discipline and lots of exercise, making them a poor match for more easy-going personalities. Their tenacity far exceeds their size, making them great guard dogs, but barking can be a real problem unless strictly controlled.

Rottweiler

Known as the "butcher's dog," this breed was traditionally used to herd the cattle and protect the day's takings after sale at the markets. It follows that they make great guard dogs. Avoid timid pups and train early to ensure a stable, even temperament. Like Dobermans, these dogs have suffered from bad (and erroneous) publicity. They are good with children but should be supervised due to their size and a tendency toward overexuberance. Food aggression can be a problem with these dogs.

One-person dogs

Chihuahua

Chihuahuas are the smallest breed in the world, which makes them easy to handle, control and groom, but they can be fairly fussy eaters. The breed originated in Mexico, and their natural dislike for the cold makes them like to snuggle up close to people or under a blanket. As one-person dogs, they can be rather aggressive toward strangers. They also have a tendency toward kleptomania, hiding stolen items in their beds.

Chow Chow

These fluffy, red dogs with blue tongues were originally bred in China for food. Fortunately, they have since become popular pets around the world, but they can be hard to train. They make excellent guard dogs because they cannot be bribed. Definitely a one-person breed, they are not always suited for families with children. If you want to gauge this quality in a potential pet, observe the puppy's parents. If they are good with their pups, chances are the pup will be good with children, too.

Maltese

One of the oldest breeds, these intelligent, diminutive dogs are extremely affectionate. Maltese make good pets for people who live alone, since they are very protective of their houses and owners. They will take on all comers. Barking can be a problem, and they can be fairly fussy with food. Because Maltese are a little headstrong at times, they are one of the breeds that require discipline.

Pekingese

Prone to laziness, Pekingese are great lap dogs. They are very affectionate and feel at home anywhere, as long as they are close to their owners. They were originally used as guards in ancient temples and can have a problem with excessive barking if not corrected early. But generally speaking, behavioral problems are relatively minor.

Shih Tzu

Not a lot is known about the origins of this breed, although it's believed that they were used as temple dogs by Tibetan monks. They are good companions for their owners, but they do not take easily to strangers and can be standoffish at times. Shih tzus are quite trainable, although their stubbornness does require patience. Despite being lively dogs, they are well suited for small living areas, as long as they have a daily, energetic walk.

Dogs with More Sociable Personalities

American Cocker Spaniel
Adorable and loving, American cocker spaniels possess a far more stable and even temperament than English cocker spaniels. However, like their English counterparts, they have a problem with excessive barking. They love the company of other dogs and people and are especially good with children.

Lhasa Apso
One of the oldest dog breeds, Lhasa apsos are known to have been bred in Tibet as far back as 900 B.C., but they were not introduced into other countries until the 1920s. They are very loving and respond well to lots of attention but do not like being left alone. Only a low level of exercise is needed, which makes them great indoor pets.

Poodle
Poodles are highly intelligent animals that are excellent with children and make fine family pets. All but the standard poodle are small in size. Their owners must educate them early in order to provide an outlet for their intellect. Poodles display many tendencies that seem almost human, like walking for extended periods on their hind legs, and they hate being left alone. They make good guard dogs, but the breed can be prone to nuisance barking if not corrected early. They are also good climbing dogs, so their fences and pens must be very secure.

Weimaraner

Selectively bred by the German nobility, these all-round hunting dogs possess some fine features. They are proud and aristocratic but also friendly, loyal, protective, and alert. Weimaraners excel at obedience training. Although they are very people-oriented and tend to follow their owners everywhere, they will occasionally fall victim to wanderlust, making good fencing a must. Some will become destructive if left alone too long.

West Highland White Terrier

These hardy little dogs are full of mischief, but their playfulness makes them a lot of fun to raise and perfect for families with children. They love company, especially that of other dogs. Quite loyal, they are also fine watch dogs. They do have a problem, however, with excessive barking.

Choosing a Crossbreed

Crossbreeds can be just as good pets as purebreds and sometimes even better. They are generally much hardier and less prone to the common hereditary faults of their purebred cousins. But certain crossbreeds are more desirable than others. Some of the more challenging characteristics in certain purebred dogs can be offset by the qualities of the breed with which a dog is crossbred. For example, a boxer's bouncy personality may be quieted by the more even character of a Labrador. While still relatively new, designer breeds generally have a combination of the traits of the breeds used to create them. It is not advisable to choose the offspring of a mix between two high-strung breeds, or you could end up with a very demanding and neurotic pet.

Some people are hesitant to adopt a crossbred puppy since they cannot precisely predict how big the animal will be when full grown. As a basic guideline, a pup is likely to inherit its size from its mother, but be slightly smaller than the largest parent.

Designer Dogs

These new hybrids of dog are not breeds in themselves. They are a cross between two purebred dogs—such as the cockapoo (cocker spaniel/poodle)—and were developed in the hopes of creating a new mix with the best characteristics of each breed. For instance, the goldendoodle combined the family friendly traits of the golden retriever with the non-shedding, hypoallergenic traits of the poodle.

These designer dogs, as they are sometimes called, are not yet accepted by the American Kennel Club, but they can make great pets. Before deciding on a designer dog, you will want to research the characteristics of the breeds making up the hybrid. Some of the more popular mixed hybrids you may have heard of are the puggle (pug/beagle), schnoodle (schnauzer/poodle), labradoodle (Labrador/poodle), chorkie (Chihuahua and Yorkshire terrier).

FINDING YOUR NEW DOG

Once you have decided to get a dog and have investigated which breeds or crossbreeds are best for you, you have several places to go to find the right animal. Many people choose to adopt a puppy from a reputable breeder who can provide you with information on the dog's ancestry, as well as the physical attributes and temperament for which it has been bred. But if you are not as particular about either and just want a good companion, consider an animal shelter. As we said earlier, each year millions of dogs are surrendered to shelters and, if not adopted, are often destroyed. Approximately one-fourth of dogs taken to shelters are purebred, but these animals tend to be adopted more quickly, and you may or may not be able to get any information on ancestry.

Choosing a Breeder

If you decide to adopt a puppy from a breeder, make sure you choose a reputable one. Good breeders will not sell their puppies to just anyone; they want all of their puppies to find the best home. Since they breed dogs for temperament as well as physical attributes, they will be able to point you to the puppy with the right personality for you.

The easiest way to find a reputable breeder is through other breeders, rescue groups, and/or your veterinarian. You can also contact the American Kennel Club (AKC) for information. Although the AKC does not endorse or recommend specific breeders, it does offer resources to find good local breeders. The AKC recommends contacting an AKC Parent Club for the breed you are interested in adopting. You can find a local club on the AKC website at www.akc.com.

Some breeders sell their puppies to select pet stores. If you decide to purchase your puppy from a pet store, check the store's references, and make sure you get a health guarantee for your new puppy. Some simply give you seventy-two hours to have a veterinarian check for any apparent medical problems, while others offer much longer guarantees, up to twenty-four months of age. This is important because some dogs do not reach maturity until two years of age and some problems do not manifest until a dog is older.

Selecting the Right Puppy with the Right Temperament

An individual dog's temperament has a lot to do with how easily it can be trained. Temperament is something a dog is born with and has nothing to do with its size, breed or upbringing. We recall one dog that had been kept in a very small box for nearly a year, receiving only enough food to live but no love or companionship. Despite this horrid experience, the dog showed no signs of timidness, only some understandable depression, after being rescued. Good training can improve certain traits in a dog, but you can never change a dog's basic temperament.

There are four basic temperament types: nervous, timid, dominant, and what we call the "middle-of-the-pack" type. Dogs with timid temperaments will respond quickly to training, while nervous types need more effort and perseverance on your part. Both of these temperaments exist in dogs at the bottom of the pack hierarchy. Dominant or strong-willed dogs are at the top of the pack and need owners that can demonstrate their own dominance through a consistent and committed effort to train their dogs, no matter how long it takes. The easiest dogs to train are those in the middle of the pack because more than anything they want to please their owners, out of respect for them as the leaders of their respective packs.

We have observed thousands of puppies over the years, and we can always spot an individual puppy's temperament in every litter, even at a very young age. It's important for you to be able to recognize temperament as well, since it has such a strong correlation to training.

If you are adopting a puppy, you can determine the temperament of each individual dog by first observing how the puppy interacts with its littermates and then when it is alone.

When the puppies are all together, watch how they run and play; focus on the differences in the body language exhibited by each puppy. This will give you an idea of where each puppy stands in the litter's pecking order. The more dominant puppies will display bossy behavior (standing over the others), and the less dominant ones will act more submissive (rolling over or lowering their height).

Then observe each individual puppy you are considering adopting alone. The first indication of a well-adjusted puppy is one that will follow you freely when you lead it away. Once alone, drop a glove or small wallet (but not one with metal on or in it) on the ground near the puppy and watch its reaction (be careful not to actually hit the puppy). A puppy that approaches immediately to investigate the object is very confident. That's a sign that this will grow up to be a well-adjusted dog, but it could be too strong willed for a more soft-natured person.

A less dominant pup will jump and move away when the object is thrown, but it will usually return fairly quickly to investigate. This reaction signals that this puppy would make a great pet and be less bossy than the one described above.

The puppy that takes a little bit longer to approach and runs around the object, acting as if it is alive and might attack, is also an acceptable pet, just a little timid. With proper, gentle training, it will grow up to be an obedient dog and a very enjoyable companion. On the other hand, the puppy that barks at the object, runs away, and refuses to return to the spot, or crouches down, could have a more nervous temperament and be difficult to have as a pet.

We also lift and hold each puppy in our arms. A pup that sits still is far more acceptable than the wriggly one. If you are looking for a very submissive type, try rolling the puppy gently onto its back, but be careful not to physically restrain it. If it fights to get back onto its feet, immediately allow it to regain its original position. If it lies perfectly still, it is the one you want.

Identifying Temperament in an Older Dog

Spending time with a dog and watching its behavior is also the best way to identify temperament in an older dog. To determine your dog's temperament, observe it with people it knows (its current owner and/or handler) and with you, a stranger. Have the owner or kennel assistant put the dog on a lead for you and then watch how the dog behaves around you and, if it is meant to be a family pet, how it acts around children. Dogs that will not get along well with children will stiffen up and try to avoid them.

Next, try moving your hands along the dog's back. A well-adjusted dog will allow you to not only pet it, but also touch its feet and tail.

You can check for food aggression by having the owner or assistant give the dog a small bowl of food. Don't try to approach the dog at this time, but watch how it behaves. Ask the owner or assistant what he or she has observed when the dog is eating.

Walk the dog on lead for a few minutes, and see if it obeys the basic commands. If it does not, the dog could still make an excellent pet with some training.

If you already own a dog but are not sure of its temperament, observe how it acts with family and friends and then with strangers. A timid dog will hold its ears back, squirm, put its tail between its legs, or roll onto its back. If your dog displays this kind of body language with strangers but

A timid dog

appears completely comfortable with you and your family, then it has a timid temperament. You can easily train this kind of dog, once it recognizes you as its leader.

It's easier to recognize a nervous dog, but there are varying degrees. For example, your dog might be quite comfortable at home but very nervous around strangers. A nervous dog might bark at a stranger approaching its property, but once the stranger actually enters its territory, it might back off behind something, like a piece of furniture, or circle the area barking and growling. Others might run aggressively and try to attack from behind. Still others will settle down as soon as the stranger is seated but then start barking and possibly try to attack the visitor once he or she gets up to leave. This type of dog is difficult to train because its fear of strangers will supersede its fear of being corrected.

A nervous dog

A dog with a dominant temperament can also be hard to control. When strangers arrive, this type of dog will put its tail high in the air, stand its ground, and, under certain circumstances, attack. An owner must be consistently assertive with a dominant dog. It will not relinquish its leadership position easily, and if you move too quickly, it could bite you. Try training the dog yourself (it all boils down to your position of dominance in the dog's mind), but sometimes owners of very dominant dogs will need professional assistance. Even the most dominant dogs can be trained; it just may take a little longer, some more expertise, and a whole lot of determination.

A dominant dog

If your dog does not fit any of the examples above, then it is a "middle-of-the-pack" type. A dog with this temperament is usually friendly toward strangers and not aggressive toward other dogs. A middle-of-the-pack dog can be easily trained and a delight to own.

A midle-of-the-pack dog

Training Guidelines for Different Temperaments

We believe that any dog, regardless of temperament, can be trained if you utilize the right approach. How easily that can be done depends, however, on your own temperament, as well as the dog's.

Just as dogs have their own personality, so do we. When our daughter asked us to pick out a puppy for her, we knew it had to be one from the top of the pack, as a timid or nervous dog would have driven her to distraction given her assertive personality. She needed a dog that she could train easily, once she had asserted her dominance, and that would not be frightened of anything. Our son's easygoing personality, on the other hand, fit better with a dog from the middle of the pack. We have outlined below how you need to respond to dogs with different temperaments and how tough you need to be to gain control.

Timid Types

You do not need to be very dominant to control a timid dog. But you do need to be consistent. Do not allow it to get away with something today because you feel sorry for it, and then correct it tomorrow for the same behavior. Timid dogs need to be trained on a daily basis. You don't need to be very forceful, just consistent with a training routine.

CASE STUDY

Crystal was a black cocker spaniel obtained from a backyard breeder. When her prospective owners went to choose their new dog, every pup in the litter except Crystal came out with its tail wagging to greet them. The couple was immediately filled with pity for the timid little creature and decided to buy her.

From the start, Crystal would cry for hours on end if left alone and would cringe with fear if anyone visited the house. As she grew older, she began growling and barking at visitors, no matter how friendly they were. Entertaining friends became a nightmare.

The owners contacted Bark Busters for help. They mentioned her timid behavior when they went to buy her at the kennels and questioned whether she might have been mistreated by the breeder. We explained that the breeder would be unlikely to mistreat only one puppy and not the others. Crystal was probably born a timid dog, inheriting the trait in the same way that humans inherit traits from parents or ancestors. As we advise in this chapter, it is preferable to avoid this sort of dog in the first place because it may develop phobias that are difficult to correct.

The good news for the owners is that that Crystal's behavior could be modified by treatment and follow-up therapy. We showed Crystal's owners how to condition and program her by getting them to place her on a lead. She tried her utmost to bite us, but we were soon able to get the owners to take control by acting in a more dominant way.

Once she understood her owners were in control, her behavior improved. She responded both to control and to praise in a manner that allowed her owners to once again receive visitors without fear of Crystal's aggression. Her so-called aggression had been masking her inner timidity and fear.

Nervous Types

Nervous dogs are always the most difficult to handle, even for experienced trainers. We found that the best approach is to be very firm; otherwise, the dog's nervousness will take over, and you will lose control of your dog. Don't expect perfection, but you can make things better as long as you are consistent and do not pity the dog.

Dominant Types

Training a dominant dog is not for the timid owner. A dog like this will refuse to be controlled by a less-dominant personality. Before starting any kind of obedience training, you will need to gain the dog's respect. Success has nothing to do with the size of the dog and everything to do with consistency and dominance on your part. A dominant owner would not walk away from a dog that growls. He or she would retaliate, not in anger, but by disciplining the dog in the manner and to the level necessary as outlined in more detail in Section Three.

CASE STUDY

One of our first dogs was a German shepherd named Monty, whose temperament placed him at the top of the pack. With proper handling and training, he went on to become an Australian obedience champion. One day, however, when he was about ten years old, I approached Monty to pick up the bone he was happily chewing. When he growled at me, I could not believe my ears. Monty had never offered resistance to me or my children touching his food. I knew I had to correct this unacceptable behavior. Using the BAH technique and other methods discussed in Sections Three and Four, I persuaded Monty to relent. Although it took some time, I knew I had to continue the correction until he stopped his aggressive behavior. He never growled at me or any member of the family again.

I later discovered the reason he was overprotective of his food. My son and daughter, who were six and seven at the time, had been taking Monty's bones away from him and giving them to our female German shepherd because she was pregnant. Nonetheless, aggressiveness is never acceptable and must be corrected immediately.

Middle-of-the-Pack Types

Although they are the easiest dogs to train, and the most delightful to own once trained, these dogs need to know that you have what it takes to be the leader of the pack. Insisting on obedient behavior is the best way to convince your dog that you are in control.

Bringing your Dog Home

Once you have selected the right puppy or dog for you, it is time to bring your new pet home. Puppies, in particular, will need time to settle in and adjust to being away from their mothers. Puppies have bonding instincts that are very similar to human babies. From birth, a pup forms strong bonds with its mother and littermates, relying heavily on the security of the family structure. Taking a puppy away from its family and then placing it in your yard or home alone can be very traumatic. An animal that is used to being part of a pack, then is forced to become a solitary animal, will suffer stress and anxiety.

CASE STUDY

Czar, a Great Dane, had been found in a shoebox as an orphaned three-week-old puppy. From the day his owner found him, she could not bring herself ever to leave him alone.

At the time, this did not present a big problem because he was very tiny and needed constant care. His owner was also lucky enough to be able to take him to work.

As he grew, however, it became difficult to take him everywhere, and the owner needed to hire dog sitters.

Czar grew very large and extremely dependent on his owner. If she went out without him, he would crash through windows to follow her. This placed a huge emotional burden on his owner, who loved him dearly but sometimes needed her own space.

We altered Czar's diet to provide a calming effect and assist with weight increase, and Bark Busters therapy was commenced promptly. With therapy, we established Czar's owner as the pack leader and reassured Czar that whenever his owner left, she would return. Training began with short separation periods that were gradually extended until Czar was no longer concerned about his owner leaving.

Just like a child, your dog needs to be educated. In the wild it would be taught to behave by the pack; in our world, it's our responsibility.

A puppy should be no younger than six to twelve weeks of age before being separated from its mother. Any younger is too soon, even if the pup has been weaned. Some breeders like to keep their puppies for up to three months in order to have a better idea of which puppy they want to keep for themselves. This is not fair to the dog because a puppy isolated in a kennel and not exposed to many people can suffer paranoia and lasting psychological damage. Early socialization, which we will talk more about later in this section, is important during the puppy's first few months of life.

When we take a pup away from its family, the whole bonding process has to start again. The pup will bond to the person who collects it from its litter, since this will be the first person it scents other than its attendant.

With an older dog, this process occurs rapidly, with the dog usually bonding to the person who leads the dog away from its old home or the shelter. Once we were asked to take a friend's dog to a breeding kennel for a mating. Throughout the day, except when she was actually mating, the dog would not let either of us out of her sight. She had bonded to us from the moment we put on her lead. Because of this powerful bonding process, prospective dog owners should try to be the person to collect the dog, whether it is a puppy or a full-grown animal.

You should bring a new puppy home early in the day, giving it plenty of time to get used to its new surroundings and new family or pack before bedtime. Like young children, your puppy will need to nap during the day. If you watch it closely, you will see when it becomes tired. Try to ensure that it falls asleep for its naps in the same place you want it to sleep during the night.

You can make the separation less traumatic for a puppy by bringing something familiar, such as a blanket or favorite toy, home with you. Put a hot water bottle (to simulate the mother's warmth) and a ticking clock (to simulate her heart beat) in its bed with a blanket to provide security. A soft, cuddly toy in a shade similar to the pup can make it think it has a littermate and is not all alone. If possible, rub the soft toy over the mother's fur to collect her scent. But most importantly, give your new puppy lots of love and human company.

The First Night

Regardless of how much effort you expend helping your puppy adjust, you will experience a certain amount of crying from the pup during the first few days. When left alone, a puppy's natural instinct is to cry out for its mother and littermates, usually due to a sense of insecurity in the absence of its pack. When this occurs, check on your puppy to make sure it is not stuck or hurt. Once you are convinced that it is safe, clap your hands loudly and growl BAH! You are letting your puppy know that you are close by but that you do not approve of its behavior. Never rush to a crying puppy to console it. In fact, if possible, it is best not to let your puppy see you during this process; just make sure it can hear you. If it sees you each time it cries, it will think that crying is the way to successfully get you to come, and it will continue to scream for attention. This process is also more effective than just ignoring the puppy and its cries. Ignoring it only leads the puppy to believe it has been abandoned, and its screams may escalate to a pitch that you cannot ignore.

Although it is difficult going through the initial separation and settling-in period, it is better for both you and your puppy to do so at this stage, rather than later when you have to go out and leave your puppy completely alone. Then, the separation for the puppy will be worse: you won't be close by to growl your correction word, and the puppy could suffer major separation anxiety.

Creating the Proper Living Space

Your dog will need a safe environment in which to sleep, eat, play and exercise. preferably It should have plenty of sunlight, fresh air, and drinking water, as well as ample shelter from the elements. Wherever you choose to keep your dog, keep safety in mind. Make sure the environment is free from sharp objects, live electric wires, and poisons, such as cleaning fluids, pesticides, and toxic plants.

The safest way to puppy proof your yard is to build or buy a playpen. Puppy playpens can be purchased from most pet suppliers, but playpens made for toddlers are also ideal for young dogs. It must be sturdy, secure and high enough that your puppy cannot climb out of it. Most playpens built for human toddlers have vertical bars to prevent climbing.

If your puppy stays outdoors, you can construct a playpen by sectioning off a part of the yard. You can also make a playpen by knocking a few stakes into the ground and covering them with strong weld mesh or a similar rigid wire that does not allow the dog to push its way out or to dig under the wire. Precast fences, such as pool fences, that are rigid and firm are also suitable. Talk to the people at your local fence or pool shop. However, make sure the fencing conforms to any local ordinances.

Sleeping Arrangements

A crate makes an ideal bed for a dog. A strong, high-sided cardboard box can be used as a short-term alternative for a puppy. Initially, leave the crate door open until your dog starts to trust its new environment.

Padded mats made out of burlap, the same material used for grain bags, make very suitable bedding material. Available at most pet shops, these mats are inexpensive and can be easily replaced if your dog chews or otherwise destroys them.

Do not think of crating as a punishment or an unpleasant thing for your dog. Dogs learn to love crates, especially if the crate is covered and it is dark and warm inside. Just like a den in the wild, a crate can make a dog feel safe and secure. Although crating can be beneficial, do not leave dogs or puppies unattended for hours on end. Nighttime is rarely a problem because most dogs just sleep all night anyway, provided that they have been allowed to relieve themselves before retiring.

Crating a dog or puppy when it sleeps is also an effective tool for toilet training. By instinct, dogs are reluctant to foul the area in which they sleep. Make sure that the crate is only large enough for the pup to stand up and turn around. Any larger and you will be encouraging the puppy to go to the toilet in a corner where it does not sleep.

Do not leave your puppy in the crate for long periods without ample opportunity to relieve itself. Otherwise, it will eventually have to relieve itself in the crate, and all of your hard work will be undone.

CASE STUDY

We were contacted one night by a Bark Busters therapist in New Zealand. He had received a call from a couple sailing around the world on a yacht with a yellow Labrador.

The dog was so well house-trained that it would not relieve itself on the boat. The owners were becoming worried about their pet because sometimes they did not sight land for days.

We told the therapist to suggest to the couple that they build a large wooden box, fill it with turf, and set it on the deck. This would be an ideal toilet for such a clean dog that had learned many years ago to go to the toilet on grass.

It worked perfectly and immediately resolved their problem.

Once you have established the area where you intend your puppy or dog to sleep, some time must be spent in training your pet to be comfortable. If outside, ensure the puppy or dog is close to the house and adequately protected from weather. A portable crate or den is a good solution, as it allows you to lock the puppy or dog inside until it becomes accustomed to its sleeping quarters. The den may then be left open during the day.

CASE STUDY

When Stella, a much-loved German shepherd, was a puppy, her owners allowed her to sleep in their bedroom. But when the dog grew older and began shedding, her owners decided she needed to sleep outside. Stella did not understand the reason for the sudden change and was frightened by noises at night. As a result of her fear, she began scratching at the door to get inside. She had totally destroyed two of them before her owners finally called Bark Busters.

Stella had felt safe in the bedroom, not outside. We recommended that her owners place a crate in a weatherproof location by the back door. By creating some noises during the day and then teaching her to go in the crate when she was anxious, Stella soon found a new safe haven where she could be comfortable at night.

OUTSIDE GUIDELINES

If you need to confine your dog outside, a good pen size is approximately 13 feet by 10 feet, if your yard size allows it. Make sure your dog's kennel or sleeping box is large enough for its size, but not too large. A kennel that is too big will allow considerable air circulation and could be too cold in winter. The sleeping quarters should face away from prevailing winds and be located near the entry gate and the dog's food and water dishes. That's because a dog will always relieve itself as far away as possible from where it sleeps and eats. If the gate is at the opposite end of the pen from its sleeping quarters, the dog will be going to the bathroom near the entrance. It's probably too expensive to reconfigure an existing kennel, but if you are building a new pen, please take this into consideration. Also, place the kennel relatively close to your house. Dogs like to be close to home.

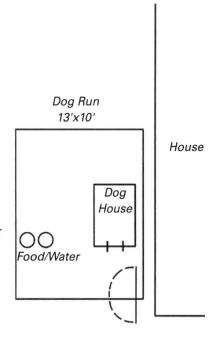

Be sure to examine your fencing. Pups and smaller dogs can escape through the smallest of holes. Once a dog knows there is a way out, you will never be able to fully confine it again. Just putting a piece of wire in the gap or a brick in front of the hole does not always work. Some puppies are very strong and can push them aside. No matter how difficult you make it, the puppy will try until it succeeds. The trick is to make the pen escape proof from day one.

If you need to put your dog on a chain, the only suitable one is a running chain, in our opinion. This kind of chain is hooked to a running wire,

which in turn is anchored between two trees or posts or from the dog's kennel to a post, with a stop to prevent the dog from wrapping itself around the post or tree. Running wires are available from most pet stores and provide a lot more freedom of movement for the dog than standard chains. It also allows the dog to relieve itself a reasonable distance from its sleeping quarters.

If you live in an area where stinging insects or wildlife are prevalent, be wary of leaving fresh meat out for your dog. Wasps have been known to land on meat and meaty bones, followed by the unsuspecting dog coming along to eat the meat. We know of several dogs that have been bitten on the tongue in this way, resulting in very painful deaths. Wildlife, on the other hand, can be attracted to the dog's food and could attack your pet.

SPECIAL GROUND CONSIDERATIONS

Slippery tiles, stairs, and uneven territory can impact the skeletal alignment of puppies and cause health problems in older dogs.

Stairs can create health issues for very young dogs, as well as for those with short legs or long backs. Puppy owners should block off stairs to prevent their dogs from constantly running up and down, which can cause back and shoulder problems. If you need a puppy or dog to go up or down stairs regularly, put it on a lead and teach it to walk slowly, executing the stairs in a sensible fashion.

A sloping yard can also cause similar problems for puppies and dogs if they are in the habit of running up and down the hill. Dog owners should restrict their dogs' access to uneven areas and fence off a more level section of their yard as an exercise area.

Slippery tiles can be equally damaging to both a developing puppy and full-grown dog. Without a correct foothold, the dog may slip and slide while trying to gain traction. This slipping can cause skeletal alignment problems. Puppies and dogs will eventually learn to walk on the tiles but possibly not before incurring some injury. If you have large tiled areas in your home, make sure your dog has an area where it can easily romp and play, without slipping and sliding.

Pool Safety

If you have an in-ground pool, make sure you keep your dog, especially a puppy, away from this area, or teach it pool safety. In the wild, if a dog or puppy falls into a pond or river, it instinctively will climb out the way it fell in; that is, as long as it is not over its head. In a pool, this instinct can get the animal in trouble.

Pools are designed with smooth surfaces that can make it difficult, if not impossible, for dogs to get a paw hold and climb out. If they follow their instincts and try to get out exactly where they fell in, they could tire and eventually drown.

To teach your dog pool safety, first lower it into the water on a long lead and then tug it gently toward the spot where you want it to exit. See if the dog can climb out unaided, or if not, make some changes that enable it to do so.

Repeat this process over and over, lowering your dog into the water at different points, but always leading it to the correct exit point. Continue this exercise until your dog automatically swims to the right spot and exits safely on its own.

Entertainment

All dogs need entertainment, but puppies, like children, require even more than adult animals. A sandbox provides a wonderful place for a puppy to dig, romp, and even rest. It can dig in the sand to find cool relief on hot days and warmth in winter.

Stock the sandbox with several safe puppy toys, such as Kongs and Buster Cubes, both of which are made of durable material and can be filled with food that your dog enjoys. The Buster Cube acts like a puzzle, providing mental stimulation to your dog as it tries to move the cube in such a way that allows access to the food inside.

Most dogs like to play catch with a ball, but be careful not to use ones that are small enough for your dog to swallow. We have heard many horror stories from veterinarians who have had to perform operations to remove balls that dogs have swallowed.

We have heard equally disturbing stories about dogs and puppies that have swallowed sticks, which then became lodged under their tongues. When thrown, sticks can land poking out of the ground. An exuberant puppy or dog could pounce on the upright stick, causing serious injury. A better choice would be to use a plastic dumbbell, available at many pet stores.

CASE STUDY

Winston, a two-year-old border collie, was playing a game of fetch-the-stick with his owner. When the dog pounced on the stick and screamed in pain, his owner took him to the local veterinarian.

The veterinarian diagnosed soft palate damage and put Winston on a course of antibiotics. But after a few days Winston began acting strangely, like a dog suffering from paranoia. He snapped and snarled at his owner from under her bed, refusing to budge from his hiding spot.

Everyone the owner had consulted advised her to have Winston put down. They suggested that his behavior was irreversible as the result of his bad experience with the stick, which he now associated with her.

When we were called in, we joined Winston under the bed. We noticed that his eyes were wild yet glazed, and he appeared to be holding his head slightly to one side. We managed to propel him into a crate, a new safe haven.

We were convinced that a physical problem was at the root of Winston's fears. A long examination revealed a two-inch stick lodged deep in his throat.

Removing the stick did not solve all of Winston's problems, as he had become chronically afraid. His therapy included a period of trust building during which he was hand-fed and walked only by his owner. Eventually, Winston fully recovered and became his old fearless self again.

Items such as hanging toys that encourage the puppy to leap and jump are not suitable. A puppy's growing bones are still soft and not yet fully developed. Constant leaping and landing can cause skeletal alignment problems and may result in the need for a doggy chiropractor to rectify the problem.

CASE STUDY

Bark Busters was called in to treat a Staffordshire bull terrier puppy named Tilly who was displaying aggression toward her owners when they tried to pet her or pick her up.

Our investigation revealed that Tilly was in the habit of leaping at a rope hanging from a tree in her play area. She habitually leaped at the rope and held on with her teeth for several minutes until exhausted. She would then let go and drop to the ground.

The puppy would do this most of the day, and her owners thought it kept her amused and out of mischief.

We identified the problem: Tilly had dislocated her shoulder. Each time she was picked up or petted, she would feel severe pain in this area. She would then try to bite whomever she perceived as the offender. A trip to a doggy chiropractor revealed skeletal alignment problems, which were quickly rectified.

The rope was removed, and Tilly's owner purchased a Buster Cube to keep the dog safely entertained.

Do not use common items, such as socks, as play toys. Your dog will have a hard time distinguishing between old socks it can play with and those you still wear.

Plastic bottles can also present problems for your puppy. Some overexuberant pups will chew these items, resulting in fragments that can lodge in the gums or stomach with disastrous results.

DIET AND NUTRITION

All dogs need good nutrition; an unbalanced or inadequate diet will create an unhappy and stressed dog. A good diet is particularly important for a puppy starting out in life. If you adopt a puppy from a breeder, most will give you details regarding the animal's dietary needs.

However, if you don't feel your dog has been on the right diet, don't make changes too soon after you bring your new dog home. A sudden diet change could cause stomach problems and diarrhea. When you do decide to make a change, don't do a complete switch all at once. Gradually increase the percentage of the new food mixed in with the old, until the new food reaches one hundred percent.

CASE STUDY

Pebbles was a twelve-month-old Shih Tzu whose fussy eating had her owners in a quandary. They had gone the "tempt-her-with-anything" road, but they were becoming increasingly concerned about the lack of vitamins and minerals in her diet. Pebbles would eat nothing but cooked ground beef, which is not a sufficiently nutrient-rich food for a dog. Her taste buds were conditioned to eating that food. If her diet were to continue, deficiencies would occur, followed by illness, bone deformities or worse.

We instructed her owners to choose a nutritionally balanced alternative. The food they selected or prepared had to contain protein, some veggies and vitamin C. These nutrients are found in meat; organs such as kidney, liver, and heart and cooked vegetables.

The owners were instructed to give Pebbles only a half portion of her ground beef combined with the more balanced food mixture. Over the next few weeks, they continued to reduce the proportion of beef in relation to the other food until she was only given the balanced diet. If at any time during the transition or afterwards she refused to eat the balanced food, they were instructed to cover her dish with plastic wrap, keep it in the fridge, and offer it to her until she ate it.

Pebbles will now eat anything her owners give her.

Some behavioral problems can be traced to a poor diet. Prepared foodstuffs on the market today provide owners with the ability to feed their dogs simple, quick meals that are nutritionally balanced. Unfortunately, in addition to vitamins and minerals, these foods often contain preservatives, chemicals, and excessively high levels of carbohydrates. Just like humans, some dogs will react adversely to them.

If you have a hyperactive dog, try eliminating these additives from its diet first to see if they are causing the bad behavior. There are plenty of higher quality dog foods on the market that contain none of these harmful additives. Be sure to check the shelf life of any food you select for your dog and make sure it can consume the quantity purchased within that time frame.

We urge you to do your homework as to which diet best meets your dog's needs. Check the label. A good dog food will have meat and a source of carbohydrates in the first four ingredients. Be wary of dog foods listing any kind of meal, such as fish meal, in the primary ingredients. Although carbohydrates are important, they should not be the first ingredient.

Vaccinations and Medication

All dogs need regular checkups and vaccinations against rabies, distemper, parvovirus and, if you plan to board your dog, for both the virus and bacteria associated with kennel cough. Keep records, as boarding kennels will need proof that vaccinations are up to date before you can leave your dog. Check with local officials regarding immunizations that are required by law and with your veterinarian as to other recommended vaccinations.

Like humans, dogs are sometimes prescribed medication for particular behavioral problems. Remember, giving a sedative to a dog (or a person) is only a temporary measure, not a cure. The only effective way to solve behavioral problems is through training.

The Benefits of Spaying and Neutering

There are a number of good reasons for neutering or spaying a male or female dog, respectively. For one, it can reduce the number of unwanted animals that are born only to be surrendered to animal shelters and possibly destroyed. Second, hormones have a significant impact on behavior and can cause both male and female dogs to act in aggressive and/or destructive ways. The best age to desex (spay or neuter) a dog is at the advent of puberty, between six and eight months of age. However, depending on your dog's health and ability to undergo surgery, it can be neutered at any time in its life. Neutering your male dog can prevent or delay prostate problems later in life, while spaying females reduces the incidence of uterine infections.

Many people are erroneously concerned that spaying or neutering will adversely impact a dog's personality or temperament. We have yet to find major differences between a dog that is reproductively altered and one that is not, except that the former may be less aggressive. A dog may put on weight after being neutered because the lack of sex hormones lowers metabolism, but this can generally be controlled through diet and exercise.

A dog with a strong sex drive can be a real nuisance. This is particularly a problem in younger dogs when hormones (testosterone in males and estrogen in females) are on the rise. The sexual responses caused by these hormones can sometimes be directed at the wrong targets: children, toys, or adult legs. Male dogs are the worst offenders, but many female dogs exhibit the same behavior. Desexing a dog is one way to prevent these problems; another is to teach the dog proper sexual etiquette through training. Even neutered animals (both male and female) may attempt to mount another dog or even a human leg, but this is meant more as a display of dominance.

Do not be alarmed if your puppy takes up sexual positions with other puppies. This is a normal form of play that allows puppies to learn about physical positioning, solicitation and rejection without risk and helps ensure normal sexual functioning as adult dogs.

An unspayed female will come into season every four to six months, during which time it can become stubborn, disobedient, and preoccupied. Male dogs can be even worse. There is no effective deterrent to an amorous male in pursuit of a female in heat. We know about one male dog that literally ate its way through a fence one week and a garage door the next just to get to a female dog in season! This persistence can result in not only an unwanted pregnancy but also a male dog running loose on the streets, exposed to dangerous situations or possibly becoming a public nuisance. A male dog can pick up the scent of a female dog in heat as far as five miles away. If two male dogs enter a rivalry for a female, both will fight to determine who wins the girl.

Males

Male dogs will do less marking, such as urinating on furniture, if they are neutered at an early age. A reproductively altered male will usually become calmer, easier to manage, and less likely to wander. Depleting a dog's testosterone level may also stop it from exhibiting aggressive behavior toward other male dogs, if the aggression is meant to display dominance. However, desexing will have little effect on a dog that is aggressive due to fear or because it was attacked by another dog.

Females
Generally speaking, people are more aware and accepting of the need to spay female dogs, but unfortunately too many also think only female dogs, and not males, need to be neutered. When animal shelters require all adopted dogs to be neutered or spayed, it's not uncommon for some people to say, "But I don't want a female dog; I am adopting a male." They fail to recognize that males are also responsible for the creation of unwanted litters. We recommend that everyone except registered breeders neuter their dogs, both male and female.

Another common but mistaken belief is that female dogs should be allowed to have one litter before being spayed. This is not only unnecessary but can also make the spaying process more difficult due to possible excessive bleeding, especially if the operation is performed while the dog is in season.

WORMING
Dogs and puppies need protection from heartworms, roundworms, hookworms, tapeworms, and other parasites that can live in their digestive tracks. Puppies that are born with worms need to be wormed early in life. There are many medications available, some that address several parasites at once. Talk to your veterinarian about which are best for your dog. You can determine if an older dog needs worming by having your vet check a fecal sample.

MICROCHIPS AND REGISTRATION
Many countries mandate that dog owners have a microchip implanted under their dog's skin. Regardless of whether it is required by law, we highly recommend this procedure. This enables authorized individuals to identify dogs

through a scanning process and can be very beneficial should your dog become lost. However, if you have had a microchip implanted and move to a different country, make sure the frequency can be detected by readers in your new community. The majority of dogs that are returned to their owners after being surrendered to animal shelters were identified with microchips, tags, or tattoos.

In many communities, you must register your dog with the local authorities and provide proof that your dog's immunizations are up to date. Check with your local city government, police, sheriff or humane society to find out about regulations in your area. Some communities also have laws regarding when dogs must be on a lead in public, while others have passed what we consider to be unnecessary laws banning certain breeds, such as pit bulls. As we stated earlier, aggressiveness is usually not the result of a dog's breed but rather its temperament and either improper or inadequate training.

THE NEED FOR EARLY SOCIALIZATION

From the time a dog is six weeks old, it should be taken to as many different places as possible and introduced to other people and dogs. This is vital for the puppy's development and to ensure it does not have fear of strangers, loud noises, or other environmental factors. Expose your puppy to traffic noises, children playing, dogs barking, and livestock running around, as well as the sounds of lawn mowers, weed eaters, and vacuum cleaners. Your puppy must learn to tolerate these everyday noises and events without chasing or barking at them.

CASE STUDY

Twelve-month-old Rocky, a German shepherd, had owners who were busy professional people. They loved him dearly, but they led hectic lives, and Rocky was forced into a solitary existence. He was lonely every day until his owners returned from work.

By the time we met Rocky, he was totally traumatized and had chronic behavior problems: his loneliness had turned him into a recluse, and he became afraid of people and the outside world. He was uncontrollably afraid of everything that moved. His owners could not even take him for a walk.

The therapy we recommended for Rocky involved getting control of him in his own yard first. Bit by bit, his owners took him closer to the gate leading to the street, and they eventually took him a little way out. We asked them to pat him continually as they walked a short distance, assuring him no harm would come to him while he was by their side. They kept encouraging and patting him until they had walked all the way around the block.

Rocky emerged from his cocoon, realizing the world outside his backyard held exciting things that were not to be feared. He enjoys his life these days, meeting people and other dogs and going for regular walks. His owners have also employed a dog walking service for him. If a dog's owners cannot find time for their dog, there are always alternatives to allowing a dog to suffer alone.

Since puppies cannot be fully vaccinated until they are four months old and the immunizations do not take effect for up to two weeks after being administered, make sure you carry your puppy in your arms when you go out in public to prevent it from sniffing the ground where diseased dogs may have walked. You should be able to visit friends with fenced yards as long as their dogs are immunized and will not act aggressively toward your pup. However, be aware that some dogs can be disease carriers without actually being sick themselves, although immunization can reduce this threat.

We disagree with the relatively mainstream belief that puppies should be allowed to play with other puppies from different litters. While puppies certainly need to learn to tolerate other puppies and dogs, we do not believe they should play with other dogs outside their immediate family unit. That's because in nature an animal's pack generally remains constant, with play related more with establishing the pack's hierarchy than with recreation. When puppies and dogs engage in what we would call "play," they are actually carrying out the equivalent of war maneuvers. It's their way of testing their opponent's strength and determining who will dominate and who will be dominated. Constantly introducing new potential rivals outside the pack will only confuse a puppy.

Care should also be taken with how you introduce dogs to one another. In a perfect world where all dog owners understand how to socialize their puppies, this would not be a problem. Unfortunately, many people do not realize the potential problems that can be caused by allowing their dogs to run up to every other dog they see. This is particularly dangerous for puppies, who will often be allowed to greet a new dog by jumping all over it. The other dog might view this as a breach of proper canine behavior and could correct the puppy for its insolence.

CASE STUDY

The story of a Great Dane named Samson demonstrates how the wrong type of socialization can cause tragedy.

Samson was a normal, fun-loving puppy until the day he ran up to a full-grown dog at the park. The dog corrected Samson for his impertinence and attacked him. From that day, Samson's personality changed. He became fearful of other dogs and would snap and growl at them if they came within reach of him, fearing a similar attack.

As Samson gained strength and height, his owner tried to keep Samson away from other dogs as much as he could. This worked well until the day a man and his Chihuahua walked into the park. The man slipped the lead off his little charge, and it bounded towards Samson and his owner. Samson immediately ran to hide behind his owner. It looked ridiculous: this giant dog was hiding from a tiny Chihuahua.

Samson's owner yelled a warning to the Chihuahua's owner to control his dog. The other man laughed, "He's only a Chihuahua. He won't hurt your dog." But before Samson's owner could comment further, Samson sprang from behind him and pounced on the Chihuahua.

This sobering reversal of behavior demonstrated Sampson's lack of socialization and the necessity of owners to have control over their dogs at all times, even small dogs. A poorly socialized dog may perceive even a small dog as a threat.

This kind of problem, whether with puppies or older dogs, is becoming increasingly common with the advent of off-leash parks for dogs. We believe these areas are great for exercising dogs, provided owners have full control over their animals and the dogs are properly immunized.

There is no easy way to introduce dogs to one another if one or more exhibit antisocial behavior. A muzzle may help until the dogs become accustomed to one another, but having control over the dogs by gaining their respect is critical.

If you have other animals in your household, introducing your new dog to them in the proper manner will be critical to how well it adjusts to its new home. A number of factors will influence how well a new dog will get along with animals already living with you, including the various animals' species, breed, size, gender, temperament, and health. As a result, it is hard to predict exactly how two animals will react to one another. Some will become immediate and lifelong companions, while others never get along well. But there are some guidelines to follow to ease the introductions.

When introducing them on the resident dog's territory, we recommend both dogs wear soft leather cage muzzles. The two dogs should also be on lead, but with the leads on the ground where they can be reached if you need to gain control quickly. Restraining a dog initially while on lead can actually cause a fearful dog to attack if it feels like it cannot get away.

Disciplining and praising your dog's behavior as appropriate will facilitate the process, especially when it comes to introducing a dog and cat. The cat will accept the dog much more easily if the dog is not allowed to act aggressively or with too much exuberance. (See more on introducing a new dog to resident pets in your household in Section Six.)

If you already own a dog and are thinking about getting another, a male and female can usually cohabit without problems. An older male dog may not readily accept another male entering its territory, regardless of age. Neutering male dogs can help, but not always. Also, never leave a young male puppy alone with an adult male; the adult could seriously attack the puppy if it oversteps its mark.

ADOLESCENCE

The majority of people experience some kind of behavioral problem with their dogs during the so-called teenage months, when their dogs are between seven and fourteen months old. Unfortunately, a large number of dogs in this age bracket have been surrendered to animal protection societies due to behavioral problems that could have easily been corrected.

The behavioral change at this age is reflective of what happens to dogs growing up in the wild. As a puppy, a dog is very dependent on its mother and the other pack members for protection and food. Generally, a puppy would not try to assert its authority over other, more mature dogs further up the hierarchy. To do so could prove fatal for a young pup that is no match for an older and much stronger dog. But as the dog reaches adolescence, it will naturally start testing the pecking order to establish its place in the pack hierarchy. Since it is vital to the pack's survival to be led by the strongest, most capable and dominant dog, the subordinate dogs will challenge the leader from time to time to make sure it has not lost its touch.

Following the same pattern, young domesticated puppies will usually do as we ask, until adolescence. Our dog's natural instinct is to test us to see where it fits in our social structure and to make sure it is as high up in the pecking order as it can possibly be. This is not unlike what happens with teenage children who begin challenging their parents' views and beliefs. We should just expect that as a dog matures, it will become more difficult to control than the little puppy that was totally dependent upon us for protection and guidance. That's why it's so beneficial to have begun training early and have established at least some ground rules before your dog naturally begins testing you. With patience and control on your part, this difficult period in your dog's life will pass smoothly.

We will discuss how to handle behavioral problems related to adolescence in Section Four.

SECTION THREE

Training Your Dog

As we learned in Sections One and Two, dogs not only feel instinctively more at ease but are also safer and better accepted by society as part of an ordered pack with a strong leader that provides guidance through discipline and praise. As your dog's owner and pack leader, it is your responsibility to provide the kind of training the dog would otherwise receive from its mother, other family members, and even siblings, depending on its position in the pack.

Dog training should begin as soon as possible. Many of the behavioral problems we are asked to correct are simply undesirable habits that dogs were allowed to form as pups. What may have been cute in a puppy can become a real nuisance and even a hazard when your dog becomes older. For example, allowing your puppy to bite your hand during play could make it difficult for your dog to understand why it is not appropriate to bite at other times. Chasing a dog can encourage it to run away rather than come when called. By teaching your puppy to adhere to certain basic rules, you can prevent many of these bad habits from forming.

But don't despair if your dog is older and has behavioral problems that need to be corrected. As we stated earlier in the book, by using training techniques based on how a dog thinks and communicates, you can correct many acquired behavioral problems; it just might take a little longer to undo what the dog has already learned. Something that takes literally minutes to teach a puppy could take a couple of hours to a few weeks for an older dog to learn.

PREPARING YOUR DOG FOR TRAINING

Before training your dog, you need to first gain its respect in order to be considered its pack leader. This process is what we at Bark Busters call "conditioning." Simply put, it involves teaching your dog to respond to a certain correction word. We've already introduced you to the word and sound we recommend: BAH uttered in a deep, guttural tone. You will need to use the same method of discipline repeatedly until the dog stops misbehaving and then reward it with praise when it does what it is supposed to do. Once you have established this as a foundation, you will know your dog is ready for training. We will discuss specifics on how to condition your dog, whether it is new to training or understands at least the basic commands, later in this section.

As a reminder, getting angry with your dog when it misbehaves will not help. Patience, consistency, and firmness will garner your dog's respect. Once it respects you, it will see you as its leader and accept your corrections. Then you will be ready to train your dog to do what you want it to do.

CASE STUDY

Clara was a well-bred German shepherd whose bad behavior baffled her owners. Her owners had bred German shepherds for twenty years and thought they had seen it all. They were bewildered when Clara began to bark uncontrollably each time they tried to leave her alone. She was inconsolable and would squeal loudly when any family member left the house or yard.

After trying everything they knew, they called Bark Busters and we interviewed them at length over the phone.

When we arrived at their home, we expected to meet an absolutely crazy dog. We were pleasantly surprised to find a dog that appeared calm and in control, with an outgoing, friendly nature. We knew instantly that this was not a bad dog, just a misguided one.

We asked the owners to demonstrate what Clara would do when they left the house. Leaving her in the backyard, they got in their car and drove off down the street. Clara went into a frenzy; she squealed and barked while pawing and scratching at the gate.

We had seen enough and signaled for the owners to come back. We began our therapy, which consisted of teaching the owners to be the pack leaders and to correct Clara for doing anything wrong around the house.

We could see that Clara had been running the household. She was rushing through doors ahead of the owners, pushing the owners with her body, and sitting in their chairs. In Clara's eyes, her owners had no pack status; she was treating them like puppies, which was the reason she behaved so crazily when they left.

Clara responded to the training very quickly. She wanted to give up control but had never been given a good reason to do so in the past. We smiled at the amazement of her owners. Clara immediately stopped barking when the owners corrected her.

WHERE TO TRAIN YOUR DOG

The best place to train a dog is in its own environment, rather than in a territory that is foreign to it, such as a training school. An unfamiliar area will create distractions and could stress a dog, both of which will diminish its capacity to learn. On the other hand, a dog that feels settled in its environment will have more enthusiasm for learning and better retention. Later, after you have prepared your dog for training and taught it some basic commands, you can conduct more specific training in other locations frequented by your dog and in situations where problems could occur, such as in a park or while walking down a busy street.

PROPER TIMING FOR TRAINING

It's critical to correct your dog at the exact moment it does something that you want it to stop. To understand why timing is so important, look at things from a dog's point of view. Let's say you want your dog to come. You start calling it, but it does not come immediately. When it eventually does, you are angry and mistakenly scold the dog, or worse yet, hit it with a rolled-up newspaper or your hand. The dog now thinks it is being corrected for coming, not for taking too long. What you should do instead is call the dog, and then if it does not come immediately, growl BAH. When your dog does come to you, even if it has taken some time, let it know that you are pleased by giving it a gentle pat and saying softly in a high-pitched voice, "Good boy" or "Good girl."

THE PROPER TRAINING EQUIPMENT

To properly condition and train your dog, you will need the right equipment. Items such as chain leads and ordinary leather collars are not effective. Below is a list of equipment we recommend. The last two items are only necessary for specific problem solving, which will be covered in more detail in Section Four.

Equipment List

- 6-foot soft webbing lead, preferably cotton or a Bark Busters training lead
- A leather or webbed collar for use when not training and to help puppies adjust to a collar for the first time
- Training collar of your choice (See recommendations below)
- Water spray bottle and "water bombs" (balloons or plastic bags filled with water) OR a Bark Busters training pillow
- 2 lightweight long leads, one 12-feet long and the other 45-feet long
- Bucket
- Cooking pot or colander

A word about training collars: Although we state that you can use a training collar of your choice, Bark Busters is strongly opposed to any collar or training aid that delivers pain, such as pronged collars. We recommend a Bark Busters training collar because when pulled taut, it makes the sound of metal on metal, similar to the sound of another dog's teeth snapping. It also prevents the possibility of choking the dog by pulling too tight or too long because the collar has a stopping mechanism that prevents choking. The Bark Busters training collar is a kinder option that is less likely to become caught or tangled on something, which could cause your dog considerable stress or injury.

USING FOOD AS A TRAINING AID

Despite its increasing popularity, we do not recommend using food as a training aid, except in certain circumstances. The mere act of feeding a dog because it has demonstrated proper behavior will not secure your necessary position as the pack leader. If that were the case, then a pack leader in the wild would only have to be a good provider to establish dominance.

The primary reason for using food in training is to create a distraction. For example, if your dog is fearful about a specific place or object, feeding it regularly in that place or near that object may help overcome its paranoia. The other time you can successfully use food to help with training is when you are teaching your dog to do tricks, which will be discussed later in Section Five.

Be careful about using food as a bribe. Bribery is often attempted by someone trying to swap an item that a thieving dog has in its possession. But this merely creates a compromise, not a cure. It will only ensure that unacceptable behavior continues and perhaps worsens. Like a child screaming for chocolate in the supermarket because he knows he will eventually get what he wants, a dog that is bribed will keep doing the wrong thing until you offer food to change its behavior. The dog is in control, not you.

The increasing popularity of using food for training can be traced to its success with animals in movies. Without someone close by offering food as a reward, many canine movie stars needed to watch the commands of their handlers offstage. When an actor has food to offer, the dogs look more natural and are content to focus on the actors. Dogs look less stilted and appear to enjoy their work. But this is a special case. Food should not be used in the majority of training situations because it is not applicable to how dogs think or act and does not establish your pack leadership.

CASE STUDY

The problem sometimes associated with the food training method is illustrated by the experience of a friend of ours with his little dog, Clipper. Clipper will perform dozens of tricks when it comes to feeding time but only then or when his owner has food. He is totally disobedient at all other times.

How to Use a Lead and Collar

We recommend that a training lead be at least six feet long because it is difficult to hold a shorter lead in a slack position. A slack lead is important because your objective is to eventually be able to train your dog off lead. The only time your pet should feel the lead is when you are correcting it. We recommend leads that are made out of cotton webbing because they have more give, are softer on the hands, and will not break easily. Chain leads may look attractive, but they are difficult to hold when trying to control a dog that is pulling. To train a dog, you will need to be able to hold on to all of the lead at some time, and a soft webbing lead is far gentler on your hands.

Puppies should be introduced to a collar as early as possible. For a first collar or one that is used when the dog is not being trained, we suggest a firm-fitting leather or webbing collar that has the appropriate width and thickness for your size dog. A good way to check fit around your dog's neck is to make sure you can comfortably fit two fingers under the collar once it is fastened.

Most dogs will scratch at their necks if they are not used to wearing a collar. It's like the first time you put on a watch. At first you will be aware that it is there, but eventually you will become so accustomed to it, you might not even notice if it were to fall off. One way to make your dog more comfortable is to put the collar on and then immediately offer your dog its favorite snack. The idea is to get your dog to associate the collar with something pleasurable.

Once your dog has adjusted to the collar, attach a light lead and allow it to drag the lead along the ground. Once again, if the dog seems concerned by the lead, you can try distracting it with its favorite food.

You can also try introducing both the collar and lead at meal time. Once you have attached both, feed your dog. Do this every day for a week, each time extending the time you leave the collar and lead on your dog.

An alternative to using food is to introduce the collar and lead to your dog during playtime. Right before starting to play, put the collar and lead on your dog. The best games to play during this time are those in which the dog chases either a ball, a toy, or you. Make sure the area you are playing in is clear of trees and other objects that may snag the lead and frighten the dog. Tug-of-war games are acceptable only if the game is not so rough that it could cause damage to your dog's teeth. Also, make sure your dog has its own tug-of-war toys. Using your own towels or clothes could encourage your dog to play with and potentially destroy your things.

Do not allow your dog to bite the lead. It might be cute to watch a dog do this, but if you allow it to happen, you may have to live with this behavior for the rest of the dog's life and that could cost you a fortune replacing chewed leads. Worse yet, your dog could become loose and put itself in danger. To stop this behavior, use the BAH correction whenever the dog tries to bite the lead.

Once your dog is comfortable, take hold of the lead and allow your dog to take you for a walk in your backyard. Do this for three days, but only walk for about five minutes a day. Always remove the lead once the time is up.

USING A TRAINING COLLAR (CHECKING)

Using a training collar correctly requires a quick, snap-release action, similar to the action of cracking a whip, known as checking. In effect, it means tightening and releasing the lead in quick succession, always leaving the dog with

a loose lead. When checking, keep your elbow straight and check straight back past your leg.

POSITIVE SIGNS OF SUBMISSION

During training, your puppy or dog may show signs of submission: head down, tail down, ears back, and tongue darting in and out. This may make you think the dog is cowering. Not so – it is actually showing you that it understands your requests and acknowledging its mistakes.

When correcting a dog, look for these signs to ensure your dog knows what you want.

Some will show the signs listed above; others may roll over or drop to the ground. Lowering of the head is a position used by both dogs and people when they are thinking. Just recall the statue of The Thinker by Rodin in which the man has his head down, resting his chin on his fist. A dog will naturally lower its head when it is thinking about what just occurred.

TEACHING YOUR DOG TO THINK

Although we can never teach our dogs to reason, we can teach them to "think." By conditioning your dog and effectively showing it what you consider good and bad behavior, it can begin to work things out for itself and correct any undesirable actions. This is what we call "motivational communication therapy." By changing the dog's focus onto the owner rather than on what it is doing, the owner has the opportunity to use the dog's language to motivate it to change its behavior, then praise it for ceasing the bad behavior.

This type of training actually turns the dog into a "thinking dog." Now, when it is about to misbehave, it will remember the distraction that occurred previously and will stop what it was about to do. Instead, it will seek praise as its reward.

Don't misread the signs of submission. Consider this example: You come home from work and find that your puppy has dug a hole. Contrary to the training guidelines taught in this book, you grab the dog, drag it to the hole, and discipline it physically. The next time you arrive home, your puppy shows signs of submission. It's not necessarily because it has done something wrong. It only remembers something unpleasant happening the last time you came back. In this case, you need to change how you are communicating with your dog, through sound and body language, not punishment.

On the other hand, if you were to catch your dog in the act of digging a hole and immediately correct it by growling BAH, your dog would display healthy signs of submission, at which time you can praise it for stopping what it was doing.

A puppy or dog that is overly submissive or groveling may be responding to an owner's body language and inability to hide his or her anger. Dogs have an uncanny ability to detect how their owners are feeling, even when they try to hide it.

If your dog shows overly submissive signs during play or other normal activities, you may be overcorrecting your animal and/or need to utilize praise more. As we have discussed, all dogs, like people, have different temperaments.

It's important to adjust the level of discipline to the dog's temperament. For example, very timid puppies may need only a minor correction (anything more could be traumatic for a young animal), whereas more dominant dogs may need stronger correction.

The best way to match the level of correction to what your dog needs is by following what we call a sliding scale of correction. By starting with a mild correction and then working up the scale until you get the desired response, you will be assured that your dog is not corrected with any more firmness than is necessary.

The Six-Step Sliding Scale of Correction

1. A low growl **BAH**

2. A louder growl **BAH**

3. A low growl **BAH** in unison with a firm clap of the hands or, if on lead, a quick check of the collar

4. A louder growl **BAH** coupled with a firm clap of the hands or, if on lead, a quick check of the collar

5. A low growl **BAH** coupled with a squirt of water from a spray bottle (or dropping a water bomb or the Bark Busters training pillow)

6. A louder growl **BAH** coupled with a squirt of water from a spray bottle (or dropping a water bomb or the Bark Busters training pillow)

The first escalation is relatively simple. You just increase the volume of your growl. This is not because your dog cannot hear you (remember, they have excellent hearing), but rather to make it pay attention to you. This is particularly helpful with puppies, which can be easily distracted.

But some puppies will still not respond to a growl alone. They have become accustomed to the growls of their littermates that carry few, if any, repercussions. By adding a firm clap of the hands at the exact moment you growl, you can add emphasis to your verbal correction and amplify the impact. Most puppies and dogs respond to the clap technique because it emulates the way another dog would snap its teeth as a correction, one they instinctively understand and respect.

Ideally, you will be able to get your dog to respond to a corrective sound only, but sometimes checking with a quick flick of the collar is more effective than clapping or easier for you if the dog is already on lead. Checking the lead with a Bark Busters training collar enables you to create a sound dogs more easily recognize and interpret as similar to teeth snapping.

CASE STUDY

Jackson was a Boston terrier that still could not walk correctly on a lead, despite twelve months of training at a local obedience school. We asked the owner to explain how she had been attempting to teach Jackson to walk correctly and what equipment she was using at the time. She said that her dog club had issued her with a leather-type check collar.

The method she was using to teach the dog to walk correctly was by snapping the lead backward and shouting the "Heel" command. But still Jackson pulled ahead, refusing every effort to get him to walk correctly.

We explained to the owner the purpose of the checking sound: why it was important and how it really works. We also showed her how a Bark Busters training collar will not choke a dog because it has a stopping mechanism that prevents it from tightening on the dog's neck. A dog reacts only to the sound of the chain being checked and will respond when the collar is used correctly. A leather check collar, which makes no noise at all, can only have the effect of choking the dog. Obviously, in Jackson's case, choking did not work.

Using the Bark Busters collar in combination with the BAH correction method, we had Jackson walking calmly at heel in just fifteen minutes, and he never reverted to his old habits again.

If your dog is still not responding appropriately, you can move up the correction scale and use a spray water bottle or a water bomb. Growl BAH and squirt the dog, preferably on the neck just below the muzzle, or drop a water bomb at its feet at the exact moment it is misbehaving. The problem with this technique is that the dog can usually see the water spray bottle or water bomb in your hand. That could lead to a situation where your dog ignores your requests if it does not see the spray bottle or water bomb. You can try holding them behind you, but some clever dogs will learn to associate your hand behind the back with the presence of the bottle or bomb, whether it is there or not.

To avoid this problem, you can use a Bark Busters training pillow. Statistics show that ninety percent of dogs will react to the sound of a Bark Busters training pillow striking the ground. When your dog misbehaves, drop the pillow close to your dog's feet but without actually hitting it. If the training pillow accidentally comes in contact with the dog, it will not hurt it because the edges of the pillow are soft. It's also easy to carry discreetly with you and access when needed.

It may be necessary to drop the pillow several times before your dog begins to respond appropriately. But as soon as it does, praise it immediately. As long as you continue to use BAH as the primary communication tool, your dog will eventually learn to respond to your voice alone.

Dropping a Bark Busters pillow is one of the best ways to correct a dog that is not on a lead. But it is not appropriate in all training situations, such as teaching a dog to sit or correcting a dog for moving out of the STAY position.

WHO SHOULD CORRECT YOUR DOG

If you ever need someone else to correct your dog, such as someone dog sitting while you are away, make sure the dog knows the person and respects him or her. To make sure, have that person go through the conditioning steps outlined later in this section. If the dog does not respect the person delivering the correction, it could become aggressive in an attempt to correct the person for overstepping his or her authority.

Children should also never be allowed to correct a dog's behavior. Children have no pack status in a dog's mind, and the dog may respond by correcting the child. (Read more about dogs and children in Section Six.)

SCENE SETTING

Given the importance of correcting a dog at the exact moment it is either thinking about or actually doing something wrong, we sometimes have to create situations where the dog misbehaves in order to train it properly. This is what we call "scene setting," and it is comparable to how more dominant dogs will teach others what is expected of them.

The benefit of scene setting is that you can teach your dog very quickly, rather than over an extended period of time. For example, think about all the times when a puppy is likely to misbehave. When you get out of bed, it may start jumping and barking at your feet. Then when you are making breakfast, it could tug at your pajamas. You rush off to the shower, only to have the puppy outside the door barking and scratching. Your puppy may also bark and start jumping up on your co-worker when he or she arrives to pick you up.

In real life, this could all happen over a period of several hours, often at times when you are not in a position to properly correct your dog. But if you had previously created situations where your dog exhibited similar behavior, you could have dealt with the misbehavior in less than half an hour. Instead of waiting for these things to happen, you set the scene. Have a friend come over on a non-workday to help when you have time to address the behavior, not when you are rushed getting ready to go to work. Have your friend walk a dog past your yard or do whatever may trigger the bad behavior you are trying to correct. Ideally, if you can stay hidden while still watching your dog, you can appear from your hiding place at the exact moment the dog begins to misbehave and correct it. After this happens a few times, your dog will begin to believe that you could always be there to discipline it, even when you seem to be away. We will use scene setting in many of the problem-solving techniques discussed later in this book.

CASE STUDY

A bull terrier always barked at a particular neighbor. Even though the owner had allowed the neighbor to make friends with the dog by feeding and patting it, as soon as the neighbor entered his own yard, the dog would bark savagely at him. So we were called in.

As luck would have it, the next-door neighbor was only too pleased to help with the dog's therapy. Together, we set the scene. The dog's owner pretended to go to work, driving his car up the road and around the corner. He then walked back and entered the neighbor's yard without his dog seeing him return.

As soon as the dog began to bark at his neighbor, the owner popped out and threw a Bark Busters training pillow near the dog, growling BAH at the same time. The dog was corrected at the instant it misbehaved and, in this way, was quickly cured.

Conditioning Your Dog for Training

Now that you have learned how to correctly use the training aids and the sliding scale of correction, you are ready to begin training your dog in a controlled environment, such as your home or backyard. If your dog does not yet obey the basic commands (SIT, STAY, DROP and COME [the Recall]), skip to the Basic Obedience instructions beginning on page 86. Your dog will be conditioned to respond to your correction during the training process. If your dog already understands the basic commands but still misbehaves in certain situations, you may want to start with the conditioning steps outlined below, and then advance to Off-Lead Training on page 98. Conditioning teaches dogs to pay attention and obey you regardless of what else might be going on around it.

Step One

Using a training collar of your choice, begin by putting your dog in a sit position and command it to STAY. Once in position, allow your dog to move its head, but the moment it moves its body, growl BAH. Then if the dog stays in position, say "Good dog" in a soft, high-pitched tone. Keep practicing the SIT, STAY, correct, and praise routine, and eventually your dog will be conditioned to stop whatever it is doing whenever it hears the BAH word.

Step Two

Your dog should be conditioned to obey you regardless of what else is happening at the time. One way to achieve this is to deliberately introduce distractions during conditioning. Introduce them in stages, beginning by crouching down in front of your dog while it is in a stay position. Then, try bouncing a ball or placing food on the ground, just out of your dog's reach. Next, ask a friend to walk into the yard or to walk another dog outside but near your property, all after you have commanded your dog to STAY. Other distractions could include children playing nearby or you running around, bouncing a ball, etc. By introducing these distractions while correcting your dog when it disobeys and praising it when it does what you want, you can teach your dog to remain steady in the stay position.

Step Three

Once your dog has mastered Step Two, the next step conditions your dog to walk through a gate or door under your direction and control. While on lead with a training collar of your choice, start walking your dog toward the gate or door. Check your dog with a snap of the collar and growl BAH if it tries to pull ahead or go through the gate. Have your dog sit at a spot just before the gate, then open it and walk through yourself, again correcting your dog if it moves from its position. Don't forget to praise your dog when it stays as commanded. Once your dog has mastered this command and is steady with the STAY command, say FREE in a normal speaking voice while pulling lightly and slowly on the lead. Eventually, your dog will associate the word FREE with the fact that you are okay with it moving from its spot.

Step Four

With the completion of Step Three, you are now prepared to work with your dog off lead. Before beginning, make sure the training area is enclosed and your dog cannot escape. Take your dog off the lead and allow it to freely investigate the area. When your dog is no longer paying attention to you, call for it to COME to you. If your dog does not respond immediately to your command, growl BAH and clap loudly. If necessary, escalate the correction according to the Sliding Scale of Correction on page 79. The instant it responds, praise it by crouching down and then standing as it gets closer. Once your dog is in reach, gently pat it while you praise it.

Some dogs will naturally want to stay near their owners even when they are off lead. In this case, you may need to set the scene to create a distraction.

You or a family member could entice your dog with a ball rolled along the ground. When the dog goes for the ball but before it reaches it, clap your hands, spray water, or drop the training pillow or a water bomb and growl BAH.

ATTENTIVENESS TRAINING

You can use the hide-and-go-seek technique to teach your dog to be more attentive to you, causing it to think, "If I don't keep my eye on my owners, they might disappear."

Select an enclosed area away from busy roadways. If you go somewhere other than your home, remember that a puppy must first be fully vaccinated to avoid the risk of contracting a disease. Begin by allowing your dog to investigate its surroundings. Once your dog is happily distracted, sniffing and exploring, hide behind something like a tree or hedge. Make sure that you can still keep an eye on your dog, but that it cannot see you.

Some dogs will panic immediately if they cannot see their owners. If this happens, do not delay; step back into view and call your dog to come. Enthusiastically praise your dog as soon as it reaches you.

Other types of dogs could not care less if you disappear. Roaming is pure paradise to them, and they will sniff and forage all day if allowed. With this kind of dog, you will need to call out from your hiding space and then wait for it to start charging about trying to find you. Next, let your dog see you and praise it as soon as it comes to you.

BASIC OBEDIENCE TRAINING

We have found over the years that most people do not ask much from their dogs beyond a few basic commands and the ability to control them in public. They want a dog that will come when called, sit still for activities such as grooming, lie down in the house or car, and stay in one place when necessary.

Most dog owners also want to be able to teach their dog to obey these commands in a matter of days, not weeks or months. The techniques outlined below will help your dog quickly master the four basic command: (SIT, STAY, DROP and COME [the Recall]) and make the time you spend together more enjoyable.

Teaching your dog to SIT

This is the easiest command to teach your dog. It is best taught while your dog is wearing a training collar and on lead, giving you full control. This is particularly important when training a puppy whose attention span is limited at best. Place your dog on your left side. Hold the lead about four inches from the dog's neck; using only your thumb and index finger, place your left hand palm down on the dog's rump. Pull the lead back with your right hand as you gently press down with your left hand. Do not push or grip this area harshly because that will tend to make a dog want to jump away from your hand.

Say SIT in your normal speaking voice, releasing the pressure as soon as the dog sits. At the same time, let the lead out and remove your hand from the dog's rump. Slowly stand up to your full height and remain standing. Do not take any steps away. If the dog stays there, praise it, saying "Good dog" in a very soft, encouraging voice. If the dog moves off the spot, growl your correction word BAH in a deep, guttural tone.

Do not rush at your dog or grab it if it moves from its position. You have the lead; the dog cannot go far. The calmer you remain, the faster your dog will learn.

Never scold a dog while you are placing it in the sit position. If you point at your dog and yell, "You naughty dog; do not move," you will only confuse your dog. Dogs learn by association, and your dog will think it is getting into trouble for sitting.

Once you get your dog to stay in the sit position, wait a couple of seconds and then say FREE, praising your dog as you do.

Repeat this exercise four times and then move on to the next exercise. It's particularly important not to overtire puppies with any exercise.

By combining the SIT training technique with the STAY command instructions below, you should be able to teach your dog in as little as five to ten minutes to sit and hold its position while you stand beside it.

Teaching the STAY Command

Successfully teaching your dog the STAY command will make handling much easier. Once your dog learns how to stay, you will no longer have to wrestle with it every time you want to put a lead or collar on it. If guests arrive at your home, you will be able to make your dog stay in a sit or down position as they enter.

We use the STAY command with our own dogs whenever we take them into or out of our house. The rules are always the same: as soon as we open any door, the dogs must sit first and wait until they are invited to come in or go out. Doing this on a regular basis will help you avoid the common problem of a dog bolting past you and through the door as soon as it is opened.

To teach the STAY command, put your dog on lead and place it in the sit position as described above. Then place your hand in front of its face, level with its nose, and say STAY in a normal speaking voice. Next, take one big step and turn your whole body to face the dog, keeping your eye on it as you move. Your hands should be locked behind your back, holding the lead. This is a subliminal signal to the dog that it should stay.

If your dog tries to follow you as you move, growl BAH at the precise moment it moves. If delivered too late, your dog could think it is all right to move, just not to approach you. By keeping your attention on your dog as you step away from it, it will get your message across more clearly.

Continue to stand still in front of your dog, ready to correct it if necessary. If it moves, calmly take it back to the spot where it started. Repeat this exercise until your dog stays on the spot waiting for you to return to its side.

You can gradually increase your distance from the dog, even to the point where you are out of its sight. But make sure you can still see your dog, in case you need to correct it for moving.

You can also try stepping inside the house while leaving your dog with its leads still on in your backyard. Wait a few moments, reopen the door slightly, and growl BAH. This will pre-warn your dog that it should not make a mad rush to come inside. If your dog moves, growl BAH and step on the lead as it runs by.

When your dog has remained in the STAY position for a minute, say FREE and praise and pat it. Your dog has done what you want and deserves a reward.

The STAY/STAND Command

Teaching your dog to STAY while STANDING will help when you need to brush or examine your dog. It's a more difficult exercise because a dog will be more inclined to wander away while standing than it would from a sitting position.

The exercise must always be done with the dog on lead at your left side, with both of you facing the same way. With the lead in your right hand, slowly move your left hand past the dog's face and bring it to rest on the dog's side farthest from you, saying STAND as you do. The hand placed gently on the side can be used to prevent the dog from sitting. Your dog will learn to associate this hand movement with the signal to stand still. With repetition, you will soon be able to communicate the same command by simply passing your hand across the dog's face and saying STAND.

Some dogs will be easier to teach this command than others, depending on temperament. More dominant dogs will naturally want to stand. All you have to do is get them to stay. The challenge is that using the correction word can cause a dog, particularly a puppy or more timid animal, to want to drop. For this reason, this exercise must be executed carefully, using a lot of praise and softly uttered voice corrections.

Repeat the exercise several times, growling softly if the dog tries to move away or sit. Do not stand up to your full height until you have practiced this exercise many times and are sure your dog understands what you want.

The DROP Command

Teaching your dog the DROP command can be useful in a variety of situations. For example, it can help you control your dog when you have guests or are eating a meal. We prefer to use the word DROP because it is not used as frequently as DOWN.

Learning the DROP command is also good for a dog. Since sitting can be a somewhat physically demanding position for a dog, telling your dog to STAY in a drop position will help prevent it from tiring. Unlike other common training techniques, we teach dogs how to drop from a standing position, as opposed to sitting first and then lying down. The movement is much smoother, which is beneficial for demonstrating obedience in dog shows. Being able to drop quickly can also help in emergency situations.

CASE STUDY

One of our first dogs, a German shepherd named Monty, might not have lived a long and happy life if not for the DROP command..

One day while we were in a field exercising him, he spotted a rabbit and made chase. It all happened far too fast for us to call him off. By the time we noticed what he was doing, he was well gone.

The rabbit quickly outdistanced him and managed to cross a very busy road. Monty was now approaching the same road in hot pursuit. We could tell that there was no way he would make it across safely; a large truck was approaching.

Then we both remembered the DROP command, and one after the other we yelled DROP as loudly as we could. We waited for what seemed an eternity. Monty was almost at the road now, and all we could do was stand there waiting for the inevitable collision.

Suddenly, we saw him skid to a halt and drop to the ground. Our training had paid off. We both feel sure that had it not been for the DROP command, Monty would have been killed that day.

To teach the DROP command, place your dog on lead and at your left side. When training a puppy, crouch or kneel down next to it; stand with older dogs. Hold the lead in your left hand or place it on the ground and step on it to prevent the dog from moving away from you. Place your left hand on the dog's back, just below the shoulder blades, fingers splayed with your thumb nearest you and with your fingers on the dog's left side. If you are holding the lead, hook the handle over and between your thumb and fingers and gather the slack under the palm of your left hand as it rests on your dog's back.

Now, place the index and middle fingers of your right hand in an inverted "V" position on your dog's muzzle. Don't worry if your hand covers a puppy's eyes. Then, rock your dog to both the left and right a few times, while saying DROP. If your dog resists, use the BAH correction word.

This technique works by causing your dog to try to see under the hand that is placed on its muzzle. As a result, it will lower itself and go into a drop position naturally. Try this exercise daily. Eventually your dog will lie down as soon as it hears the DROP command, without any physical assistance.

Once the dog starts to move downward, praise it. You can lift your hands off your dog and only need to reposition them if the dog tries to get up. When it drops to the ground, stand up straight beside it, and be ready to correct it if it attempts to stand up without a command from you. It should remain in the drop position until you say FREE.

Teaching Your Dog to Come When Called: The Recall

Teaching your dog to come when called, what we refer to as the Recall, is a critical skill. After all, if your dog will not come to you when you call it, trying to teach it any other commands will prove useless.

Although it is never too late to teach a dog to come, the best time for training is before a puppy is six months old, when it is still dependent upon you and less likely to wander far. If a puppy is given too much freedom and allowed to explore off the leash, it will soon find adventure. An owner will be no match for the enticement of new scents and unexplored territory.

Then, if the pup bounds away rather than coming when called and its owner begins to chase it, the pup will think, "Hey, this is great. We are all following the scent (or chasing a cat or whatever caught its attention at that moment)." The puppy cannot understand that it is misbehaving; after all, the pack leader is joining the chase. The right response from the owner would have been to stand still or, better yet, run in the opposite direction. As the pack leader, you should always be in the lead and never the one to chase a dog.

This is a relatively easy skill to teach, but it requires careful use of your voice tone and a few additional training aids. You will need two longer leads: one 12 feet long for working in your backyard and one 45 feet long for times when you venture to places with more space. Both leads should be lightweight to ensure that the dog does not feel them when they are held slack. Both leads should have a clip, which can be attached to the dog's collar, and a comfortable handle.

You can easily make your own leads with items purchased from your local hardware store. You will need a strong clip that snaps shut automatically, much like the connecting clips used by mountain climbers but in a size suited for your dog. A mower cord makes a good lead, but we suggest you use gloves while training to avoid any injury to your hands. Attach a handle made out of a leather strap or pieces of an old handbag. Whatever you choose to use for the lead cord and handle, both should be strong and durable.

This exercise should first be tried out in your own backyard using the shorter lead, then in your front yard, before trying it in a public place. Start in an enclosed area, if possible. Place your dog on the lead and grip the handle. Now, walk around the yard, with the excess lead trailing on the ground. Don't worry if it becomes tangled under the dog's legs; most dogs will manage to step clear. However, if the dog becomes impossibly caught up, stop and untangle the mess.

Each time your dog strides ahead of you or investigates something, tug and then release the lead and growl BAH until it turns to move in your direction. Then, still holding onto the lead, let it go slack, crouch down, and tell your dog to COME. Pat your leg to encourage it to come to you. Unlike other commands, this one should always be delivered in a very pleasant, as opposed to normal, speaking voice, in order to be more inviting. Once your dog comes to you, pat it as you straighten up to your full height. Repeat the process several times.

Teaching a Distracted Dog to Come When Called

Most dogs willingly come to their owners when called if there are no other distractions. But once something more interesting comes along, such as another dog, a cat, or some food, the owner is fast forgotten. Here's how to make sure your dog comes whenever called, regardless of what else is happening around it.

With your dog still on the lightweight lead, throw its ball or favorite toy. Allow it to chase the toy five or six times and enjoy the game. Then, the next time, stop the dog's progress toward its ball or toy by standing on the lead and growling BAH. Now crouch, encouraging your dog to come to you by saying its name, followed by the command COME uttered in a soft, inviting voice. Praise the dog as soon as it arrives at your side.

If your dog is charging after an object or another animal, you must be able to stop it in its tracks by growling BAH, and then tell it to COME. Using the correction word before the command will speed up the learning process. The dog does not need a complicated set of instructions, only the correction word to communicate it has done something wrong and should cease what it is doing immediately. Eventually, just by hearing the word COME, the dog will stop and return to you.

If your dog refuses to respond to the correction word and persists in running after the ball, just keep saying BAH and tugging on the lead. Be persistent; if you cannot stop a dog from chasing a ball, you will never succeed at stopping it from chasing anything, such as cars or other animals. With this technique, you can also let your dog play ball for awhile, say five or six times, and then get it to stop on the seventh throw.

Once you have successfully used this pattern, change it. Sometimes allow your dog to chase the ball only every other time; then another time stop your dog on the first throw. Just make sure, as you are varying the pattern, that you let your dog chase the ball enough to keep it interested in the game.

When teaching your dog the Recall, it is not enough to use just the dog's name. We regularly come across people who try commanding their dog to come by calling them by name only and then wonder why they don't obey. We show the owners how fruitless this can be by calling them by name, over and over. They stand there, responding "Yes" each time we say their names. They have not realized until now that, if we call a person using his or her name only, the person cannot possibly know what we want, least of all that we want them to stop and come running to us. It's no wonder that their dogs will not come to them when they call.

WALKING YOUR DOG ON LEAD

Going out for a walk with your dog can be a delightful experience for both you and your dog, or it can be a battle to lead the way, which the dog almost always wins. We've seen owners employ all sorts of techniques to gain control: from literally digging in their heels, to grabbing tree branches as they pass, to wrapping the lead several times around their hands. The problem is dogs are natural pullers and if they feel restraint of any type, they will only pull more. Just think of sled dogs and you can imagine how the techniques listed would only make problems worse. As one owner described his experience, "When I take my dog, Toby, for a walk, I place him on the lead, look at him, and say, 'Where are we going to go today, Toby?' "

Whether you are teaching your dog for the first time how to walk on the lead or correcting problems such as too much pulling, the BAH correction method is the quickest and easiest way. If you praise your dog as soon as it stops pulling, it will also learn that it should walk calmly at your side.

Start the training in your backyard, where your dog has already sniffed everything and will not be as distracted by new scents on the street. You will need a properly fitted training collar and a six-foot long webbing lead. Place the dog on lead, and anchor the lead by securing it firmly in your right hand and gathering up any slack in your left.

Now, with your dog on your left side, start walking. Your dog's front legs should always be level with your legs. Praise your dog in a soft voice, and pat its head gently when it is in the correct position.

Be sure to hold the lead loosely, checking and then quickly releasing it. A taut lead will only encourage your dog to pull. Keeping the lead loose will also make it hard for your dog to know if it is on or off lead, which will help the transition to off-lead training.

Each time the dog pulls ahead, check it by making a backward motion with your left hand. Since the dog has taken up all the slack in the lead by pulling, you will first have to slacken it by moving your hand forward and then snapping it backward. Keep your elbow straight, bend your body forward, and come to a momentary halt as you check straight back past your leg, growling the BAH correction word at the same time. Then as the lead becomes taut, immediately release the lead in your left hand. Praise your dog the moment it responds.

With a Bark Busters training collar, checking and releasing the lead will create the clinking sound that will make your dog respond. Then, once the dog hears the sound, you can release the lead, which in turn will discourage the pulling.

When the lead is loosened, the dog may at first try to run farther away from you, but if it is immediately checked, your dog will avoid the same thing happening again. The next time the lead is loosened, it will learn to stay at the same spot, next to you.

Never correct a dog verbally or by checking for lagging behind. If you do, you will only make it drop back further. Start patting your leg instead; this gesture is seen by a dog as encouragement. Praise it as soon as it comes up beside you. Say "Good dog," in a pleasant, high-pitched voice.

If you are walking a puppy and it suddenly stops, throws itself on the ground, and refuses to go any further, do not try to drag it. That will only traumatize the puppy, making training much harder. Try flicking the lead a couple of times to see if that encourages the puppy to keep going. You can also try holding some food just out of the puppy's reach. If this does not work, contact your local Bark Busters therapist. When training a puppy, don't overdo it. Over-exercising puppies under six months of age can cause skeletal damage.

Using the method, you should have your dog walking correctly on the lead in about an hour, maybe less. In the early stages of training, you will probably need to do minor maintenance, performing reminder checks (check-and-release while growling BAH) each time you take your dog for a walk.

If your dog refuses to walk correctly on the lead, try one of these two corrective measures:

1. Take your dog to a strange area and put it on lead. Ask a helper to hold the dog's lead while you walk about thirty paces away. Crouch down and call your dog. Then, ask the helper to slowly walk your dog toward you, mildly restricting it by holding the lead back. Keep saying COME in a soft voice until they reach you. Practice this several times over a period of a few days. Eventually the dog will walk forward on its own when you say COME. Then, once the dog is walking on lead, use the technique above to correct it when it pulls.

2. Place your dog on lead. With a piece of chicken or another tempting morsel in your right hand, hold the lead in your left and say COME. Bring the food close to the dog's nose, but move it forward again to encourage the dog to take a few steps. Praise it when it does. Keep

repeating COME to teach your dog that this is the command it will need to respond to once you stop using food as an incentive. As your pet steps forward, continue to reward it. Then, once your dog is walking properly on its lead, use the check chain to stop it from pulling and discontinue using the food.

Off-Lead Training

Preparation for walking off the lead

Do some preliminary work before taking your dog off lead. Make sure your dog reliably stays in the correct position as you walk it with the lead, using the BAH correction word if it starts to rush ahead or becomes distracted. Praise your dog with a soft melodic voice as soon as it comes back in position. Continue doing this for a few days or until you can keep your dog reliably at heel using only your voice. You must be confident that your dog will respond to your voice before you take it off lead.

Being able to control your dog off lead does not happen overnight. However, if you have followed all of the preliminary exercises outlined in this book, you will be able to progress to off-lead work relatively easily.

Controlling your dog off lead

A good way to start gaining control of your dog off lead is to let it run free while making it think you still have it on lead. You can do this by letting go of the lead when you are in an enclosed park or field.

Allow your dog to move away from you. Next, crouch down and encourage your dog to come back to you, and praise it as it approaches. Growl BAH if it stops on its way or deviates from the most direct path to you. Repeat this exercise several times until your dog responds immediately when you growl the correction word.

Now ask a friend or relative, someone the dog knows, to help you. Have your assistant lead the dog a short distance away from you, keeping it on the lead. Instruct him or her to move approximately ten feet away the first couple of times, and then progressively farther as the dog proceeds through this exercise. Discontinue this exercise if the dog displays any adverse reaction to being led away from you.

Once your assistant has led your dog away, growl BAH and clap. Instruct your assistant to let go of the dog.

If you follow these steps, your dog should respond every time you call it. When this happens, you are well on your way to having a dog that can be controlled off lead.

Teaching your dog to walk correctly off the lead

Once you have trained your dog to walk correctly on lead and prepared it for off-lead work, the transition to having your dog walk correctly by your side off lead will be easy for both of you. The only condition for success is maintaining the same body language as you used in the earlier exercises.

If you have been holding your hands a certain way when grasping the lead, then they must be kept in exactly the same position during off-lead training. There are two reasons. First, since dogs learn by association, they will respond to you exactly as they did before if they see you in the same position. Second, if your hands are in a different position now that the dog is off the lead, it may soon realize that you are no longer holding the lead.

Leave the training collar on your dog and remove only the lead. Instead, attach a shorter version of the lightweight cord you used to teach your dog to come when called. This shortened cord is designed to be used if you need to gain control of your dog quickly.

It will also make the dog believe it is still on lead.

Start training with your dog sitting by your side. Step off on your left foot, and say WALK in your normal speaking voice. If your dog just sits there or lags behind, crouch down with your body still facing forward and encourage the dog to follow. Most dogs will approach faster if you lower your height.

If your dog lags behind, do not correct it, verbally or by checking. A correction will only make your dog drop farther back. Pat your leg instead, as this gesture will be seen by the dog as encouragement. Praise it as soon as it comes to your side, saying "Good dog" in a very pleasant voice and high-pitched tone.

Don't always pat your dog when praising it. You want the dog to become accustomed to voice praise only, which is necessary for those times when you are working off lead and your dog is some distance from you. You don't want to have to run up and pat your dog every time you want to praise it. That would only make you do extra work and create a distraction for the dog.

When your dog walks correctly at your side, praise it with your voice and keep walking. If the dog races ahead, passes you, or deviates to the side, growl BAH, and then praise it the moment it responds.

Make sure you walk in a straight line; otherwise, you risk bumping into your dog. Introduce some turns as part of a pattern, for example, a right turn, followed by a left turn, followed by an about turn to the right, and then one to the left. To avoid tripping over your dog when making a left turn, lift your right knee as you turn, gently guiding your dog out of the way. Do this until the dog gets used to these turns.

Continue these walking patterns for about ten minutes, using the BAH correction each time that your dog bounds around, steps out of position, or makes a mistake. Praise it with your voice as soon as it corrects itself. During this time, have a friend walk alongside and try to distract the dog in a pleasant way, such as crouching down and vocally encouraging the dog in a high-pitched voice, saying "Good dog." This should serve as sufficient distraction during the training stage; rapid movements could upset the dog, slowing down its learning capacity.

Introducing distractions teaches your dog to focus on you, no matter what else is happening around it. Many people tell us that their dogs are very cooperative at home but refuse to do anything when they are in public. That's because distractions were not properly incorporated into the training process.

After a couple of sessions with your friend distracting your dog, ask another person with a friendly dog to help in the same manner. Training with other animals as distractions will teach your dog to be calm in their presence, rather than preferring to play with or approaching the other animals.

This off-lead training technique—introducing as many distractions as early as possible—is designed to get your dog to use its brain as early as possible in the process and therefore learn faster.

Recalling Your Dog Off Lead

As the popularity of dogs as pets has increased, the restrictions placed on dog owners have increased as well. It is our responsibility to ensure that we can control our animals in public. Too few owners take the time to train their dogs, and when an untrained animal is unleashed for a run, the trouble starts. If the dog were to try to attack another dog or a child, its owner will have little chance of stopping it before someone or something is hurt. If we want to permit our dogs some freedom, then we need to be able to call them back to our sides at any time. It is vital that our dogs respond immediately to our commands, no matter where they are or what is happening.

To test your dog's readiness to come to you when called off lead, go to an enclosed park or field, rather than your property. Before letting your dog off lead, make sure it cannot escape and that there are no people or dogs in the area. Leave the training collar on and let your dog off lead. Give your dog time to explore its surroundings, then call it to COME. Crouch and praise your dog as it approaches, standing and patting it when it reaches you. If your dog ignores you, growl BAH and utilize one of the suggested training techniques from the Sliding Scale of Correction on page 79. Repeat this until the dog responds appropriately, remembering to change your tone of voice as soon as the dog obeys.

Owners need to display Dr. Jekyll and Mr. Hyde behavior, acting in a dominant manner (standing tall, growling) when correcting their dogs and submissively (crouching, soft voice) the moment their dogs look at them or show any interest in what they are doing or saying. Some dogs will respond the first time; with others, you may have to use the selected correction aid or technique twenty to thirty times before the dog gets it. Repeat this training every day for a week until your dog responds in a reliable manner. You won't know how quickly your dog will learn until you start, but keep trying until your dog comes to you.

TRAINING YOUR DOG TO RESPOND IMMEDIATELY

If you want to train your dog to come back to you as soon as you call it, whether it is on or off the lead, follow this important guideline: Give the command, followed by the one word correction as necessary. Do not keep repeating the command over and over. Say "Rover, COME, BAH. Rover, COME, BAH," as opposed to just "Rover, COME. Rover, COME." If you consistently correct your dog as needed, it will soon learn to respond immediately, rather than waiting until it feels like it. Consistency at this stage will yield dividends later when you could be in an emergency situation that requires your dog to obey you instantaneously.

Teaching RECALL from the SIT/STAY position

Place your dog in a SIT position, this time keeping your hands locked in front of you and your eye on your dog as you walk approximately ten feet away. Stop and face your dog. Wait ten seconds, then call your dog by name followed by the command COME. At the same time, raise your hands over your head. This will become the dog's signal to come to you. Similarly, your hands locked in front of you will be the subliminal sign for your dog that a recall command is coming.

If your dog starts approaching on command, slowly crouch down and encourage it to come further by patting your leg. If your dog has a tendency to overshoot you because of its speedy response, stand against a wall. Because it will not be able to pass you, it will become accustomed to stopping when it reaches you. Praise your dog lavishly when it arrives at your side and gently place it into the sit position, but this time do not say SIT. If you repeat these steps enough, your dog will soon learn to sit when it comes to you.

You can encourage a dog that does not move to approach you by lowering your height or running backwards as you say COME. Praise the dog as soon as it starts moving toward you and again when it finally reaches you. If your dog still refuses to budge, don't be harsh. It's not stubborn, just confused. Some dogs mistakenly think they shouldn't move once they are in the STAY position. Attach the shorter lightweight lead, and gently check your dog toward you. This entails tugging on the lead in your direction, tightening your hold, and then loosening it.

Preventing Your Dog from Anticipating Your Call

Vary how you call your dog from a sit/stay position to prevent your dog from anticipating your command and starting to move as soon as it hears its name. The best way to prevent this from happening is to call your dog by name, followed quickly by STAY; at other times, call the dog's name first, then say COME. By changing the order, the dog will not know what is coming next and will learn to listen for the actual command before responding.

TEACHING YOUR DOG THE FINISH COMMAND

Some owners, particularly those who show their dogs in competitions, prefer that their animals go directly to their left side when recalled, rather than coming and sitting in front of them. The owners consider this preferable because they need their dogs to walk off with them immediately, although some countries' trials regulations state that the dog must first come and sit in front of its handler and then go to the heel position. Regardless of the exact rules, this is what is known as the "finish."

If you want to teach your dog to go directly to your left side, simply put your right hand down to pat it. At the same time, guide its rump with your left hand, bringing it to the desired position facing in the same direction as you, on your left side.

Using another technique, you can get your dog to go straight around your right side, ending on the left. Attach the small lightweight cord; then, as your dog approaches in the recall position, gently take hold of the cord and step backward. Take one step forward as you guide your dog around to your left side, and swap the cord from your right hand to your left hand as you guide it into the sit position.

For both of these techniques, there is no need to give any command other than COME, as the goal is to get the dog to complete the exercise according to your preferences with just one command.

To teach the FINISH command, attach the 16-foot lightweight lead to your dog's collar, then command it to COME from the sit position. Then, when your dog comes to you, pat it gently while taking hold of the lead with your right hand. Say the command FINISH as you take one step back and then one step forward. At the same time, swap the cord to your left hand and bring the dog around to your left side. Praise it as you make it sit.

You have now learned how to condition your dog to respect you as its pack leader and teach it basic obedience. But even well-trained dogs can develop specific behavioral problems. Read on to learn why dogs misbehave and how you can use what you have learned so far to diagnose the cause and correct the problem quickly and easily.

Correcting Problem Behavior

In this section, we will provide specific techniques for correcting some of the most common behavioral problems. To get the most out of this section, make sure you have already read Section Three and understand the principles behind the Bark Busters training method and the selection and use of various corrective training aids (the water sprayer, water bomb, and Bark Busters training pillow). Further, by reading Section One on how dogs think and learn and what causes certain behaviors, you will be able to more easily determine how to apply the training techniques to a wide variety of problems.

CORRECTING PROBLEMS CAUSED BY AGGRESSION

Many of the problems we are asked to correct have to do with aggression. Aggressive behavior against you or any member of your family must never be tolerated. Even seemingly minor aggression, such as growling from time to time, should not be ignored, as the aggression will likely escalate if uncorrected. A growl from a dog is a warning that if you keep doing a certain thing, the dog will bite. For example, if a stranger enters a dog's territory, the dog may start snapping, snarling and barking. Some dogs will launch a frontal attack, while other, less confident dogs will circle and try to go for a rear attack. In most cases, if the owner tries to intervene, the dog will believe it has backup, which will only give the dog more confidence and incite it more. The result? The stranger will likely be bitten.

WHAT MAKES SOME DOGS AGGRESSIVE?

One of our favorite sayings is, "You can take the dog out of the wild, but you cannot take the wild out of the dog." This means simply that the dog's natural instincts are never far below the surface, and sometimes this behavior can manifest itself as aggression.

One breed of dog is not necessarily more aggressive than any other. Bark Busters therapists have treated all breeds of dogs for aggression and found that the diminutive Chihuahua can be just as aggressive as the much larger Rottweiler or German shepherd. The only real difference is that the larger dog can instill more fear in us because its size and ability to cause more harm.

Aggression in a dog must be dealt with firmly. Unfortunately, many dogs are put to sleep for behavior problems that could have been corrected. To address aggressiveness in your dog, you must first gain its respect and second understand the root cause of its aggression. The cure you employ will depend in large part on what is causing the dog to behave the way it does.

If your dog is acting unpredictably—friendly one minute, aggressive the next—it will be hard to predict when you will need to correct it. In this case, the first thing you need to do is make sure that your dog has developed full respect for you. You can achieve this subtly by establishing dominance in a passive manner, as outlined below. If your dog is only testing your authority, then simply spraying water or dropping the Bark Busters training pillow, combined with the correction word BAH, might be enough to get your dog to refocus its attention and obey you.

In either case, be very determined when correcting aggressive behavior. The problem will not go away on its own. Conditioning your dog daily can help prevent aggressive behavior because it reinforces your dominance over the dog and increases your ability to control it.

ESTABLISHING DOMINANCE IN A PASSIVE MANNER

Dogs in a pack situation will sometimes establish leadership in a very subtle way through body placement and gestures. By always being the first to enter the den, never taking a backward step when challenged, never walking around another dog, and always leading the group, a dog sends a message to other members of the pack that it is the leader. Through their actions, many dog owners we work with have been telling their dogs the exact opposite, that they are the subordinate ones. Owners send this message by walking around their pets when the dogs are blocking their path, or when they allow their dogs to enter rooms before them or let them go first up or down stairs. To a dog, these are all subliminal signals that its owner is subordinate.

Then, when the dog asserts its dominance by attacking another dog or human, its owner is astounded. But he or she shouldn't be. All along, the owner has been subliminally telling the dog that it is the leader and, therefore, the one making all of the decisions for the pack.

To regain dominance in a passive manner, an owner must display leadership qualities in a consistent manner as outlined above. In addition, never walk around your dog; make it move out of your way. Never go to your dog; ask your dog to come to you. Never chase your dog; remember, the leader always leads.

If you adhere to these rules, your dog will begin to view you differently, as its leader, and it will be less likely to challenge your authority.

Aggression Caused by Fear

The most common cause of canine aggression is fear of the unknown; that is, whatever the dog cannot understand or does not recognize as normal. Fear can then manifest itself as aggression in the form of driving off the unknown intruder or object. Once the object of the dog's aggression has gone, the dog will view this as a victory and will only become more aggressive the next time, convinced that its actions successfully removed the object of its fear.

If a dog is not properly socialized, it can become fearful when it meets strangers or other dogs for the first time. Fear and a dog's response are instinctual. When a dog becomes frightened, it will do one of two things: fight or take flight. A dog that has not had contact with other humans or dogs or that has been traumatized by another person is more likely to attack than one that is well socialized.

CASE STUDY

We were called in to help with an eighteen-month-old Belgian shepherd named Bear, who had suffered a frightening experience as a young pup. When Bear was four months old, a man entered Bear's yard to scare out some stray dogs. The man acted with great aggression, kicking and chasing the dogs as Bear watched in terror. From that time, Bear feared that he would receive the same kind of treatment from all strangers, and he would attempt to attack anyone who entered his territory.

When we arrived at Bear's house, we were met by an onslaught of barking and growling even though Bear's owner tried to quiet him by yelling "Bear" each time he leapt at the door. We asked her to open the door, and she was horrified as Bear charged at us. But he stopped short, barking madly as we stood our ground. He jumped back and forth noisily. We noticed that each time he backed up near his owner, she would attempt to console him by patting him and speaking reassuringly. The problem was that the dog interpreted this as support for his antics and thought he was being praised for acting aggressively.

We handed a training pillow to Bear's owner and instructed her to drop it near the dog's feet and to growl BAH when he next lunged at us. After only two attempts, Bear ran outside, after which his owner told him softly that he was a good boy. Bear ran to her for a pat and then sat in front of us and offered us his paw. The owner could not believe her eyes, but that was nothing compared to our disbelief as we had never seen a dog do that in all of our experience.

Often we are called in to help with dogs that have exhibited fairly long-term aggressive behavior. But a situation may also arise where a dog that is normally happy and outgoing suddenly becomes aggressive for no apparent reason.

Some dogs are simply born with a more fearful temperament, while other less dominant types may become afraid if they sense they do not have a strong leader. If their owners do not display sufficient leadership qualities, the dogs feel vulnerable and take matters into their own hands to protect themselves.

Aggression toward Other Dogs

Dogs in the wild would drive off any other dog or marauding animal that approached the pack or its territory. Today, many owners expect their dogs to behave in a friendly manner toward all other dogs that come along, but some individual dogs, as well as some breeds, have a stronger instinct to protect the pack than others. I have found that German shepherds, greyhounds, Welsh corgis, Australian cattle dogs, Rottweilers, and terriers of all kinds have a very strong pack instinct that can be both a positive and a problematic trait.

The early socialization of a dog is critical if it is to establish good relations with other dogs. (See the "Importance of Early Socialization" in Section Two.) A submissive dog may never have a problem with other dogs, choosing instead to demonstrate immediately that it is no threat by squirming or groveling, holding its tail down or between its legs, averting its eyes, and pulling its ears back or flat against the head. Other dogs will immediately look for signs to establish which animal is most dominant: the stronger dog will hold its tail high over its back, stand as straight and tall as it can, and move with a definite, rigid gait.

A dog that is aggressive toward other dogs may pull at its lead, trying to engage in battle with the other dog, or it may run up and down behind a fence, barking and growling at another dog passing by. To gain the upper hand, you must first have established leadership over your dog. Conditioning should be carried out for at least two weeks before any attempt is made to control the dog's aggression. (See more on "Conditioning Your Dog for Training" in Section Three and "Establishing Dominance in a Passive Manner" in this section.) Only after the dog is obeying you as a result of the conditioning can effective treatment be administered.

Treatment must be conducted in a controlled environment, such as your own backyard. Have a friend walk another dog up and down the other side of the fence. Let your dog run free in your yard, with no lead on. Use one of the training tools discussed in Section Three (water sprayer, water bomb, or training pillow) and growl the BAH if the dog starts acting aggressively toward the other dog. The treatment will have to be repeated over a couple of weeks, with you dropping the water bomb or pillow approximately five to six times each session. Make sure the dog is cured before attempting the same thing in public. When you do treat the dog outside your home, make sure it is on a lead. You will need to give a very strong correction, utilizing the BAH word and a solid check, to make sure your dog knows you are very displeased with its actions and to draw the attention of the combative dogs away from each other.

AGGRESSIVE BEHAVIOR WHILE WALKING YOUR DOG

If your dog exhibits aggressive behavior toward other people or animals while you are walking it, ask some friends to help you. Ask one friend to walk a friendly dog down a street toward you. Have another friend, someone your dog knows and respects, walk behind them, out of the dog's sight. Walk your dog as close as possible to them, without putting anyone in danger. As soon as your dog begins to act aggressively, have the person in hiding pop into sight and correct your dog by growling the BAH word and using one of the recommended training aids. Because your dog cannot reason, it will think that your friend is always hiding behind anyone who walks down the street. Don't forget to praise the dog once it stops being aggressive.

Do not allow your dog to retreat after being corrected. Many nervous dogs, once they have been cured of aggression, will attempt to move away from you, other dogs or people. People mistakenly believe that this is cowering. It is actually the dog's true personality, which had been masked by the aggression. This new response should also be corrected, using the BAH word and, if necessary, the water spray bottle or training pillow. Otherwise, your dog could spend the rest of its life running away from strangers. At the same time, don't expect a nervous dog to ever be overly friendly.

CASE STUDY

A twelve-month-old Rottweiler, Ghengis, had been a well-adjusted animal up to the age of about five months. Then he was attacked by
another dog. The other dog's owner finally arrived and beat the dog off
both Ghengis and his owner. This incident had made Ghengis aggressive toward other dogs, as well as other people. He was now a highly
disturbed dog with very antisocial behavior.

When Bark Busters was called to treat his problem, Ghengis tried
several times to bite us. The nature of the prior attack had made Ghengis
think that both the other dog's owner and the dog were attacking him.
He thought his only defense was to "get them before they get me."

He also thought that he was protecting his owner as well as himself
by his aggressive behavior. To him, the attack had been made on both
of them, and we were sure he felt his owner now condoned his violent
actions.

The best way to cure Ghengis was to have his owner first correct him
for his actions. Her fear of the attack had probably contributed to his
problem because she would tighten the lead when other dogs
approached. This became a signal to her dog to be aggressive.

We showed her how to be his pack leader. We gave her a training pillow and instructed her to bring Ghengis into the room and to drop the
pillow near his feet, growling the BAH word, followed quickly by praise
as soon as he reacted. As soon as she led Ghengis in, he started barking and growling and lunging at us. She quickly dropped the pillow and
growled as instructed. Ghengis immediately responded by sitting down
and looking at his owner in disbelief. She patted him lavishly, but he
began barking and growling at us again. She picked up the pillow and
repeated the process. He responded in the same way.

We continued the training for about fifteen minutes, until he was no longer acting aggressively toward us. We then offered him some doggy treats and finally had him eating out of our hand. Once he realized that his owner was not happy with his actions, he was quite content to accept us. His owner would now have to repeat the treatment with other people, correcting him for any aggression.

However, the treatment was far from complete. We still had the aggression toward dogs to address. Starting with a controlled situation would minimize the dangers. We arranged for a friend to walk her dog close to Ghengis's fenced yard. When Ghengis began misbehaving, we used the training pillow as before. It took many corrections to stop him because we were dealing with fear, but Ghengis finally responded to the BAH word alone.

We then faced the biggest challenge of all: going back into the street where the trauma had occurred. By now the owner was able to handle Ghengis more confidently, and we showed her how to condition and program him. He proved to be a very responsive and highly intelligent animal. In no time, he was walking by his owner's side on a loose lead, sitting, staying, and dropping on command.

Finally, we had the owner take him into the street; she carried the training pillow for back up. Every time Ghengis would step forward or pull on the lead, the owner would correct him. This made him very calm. He now had to concentrate on his owner, rather than what was going on around him. He ignored people who walked past, reacted to one barking dog, and finally, after being corrected several times, ignored all other dogs as well. Ghengis's cure was complete.

This type of aggression can be highly dangerous and in some cases professional help and assistance will be required.

IF YOU ARE CONFRONTED BY AN AGGRESSIVE DOG

If you are walking your dog and another aggressive dog is running toward you, do not stop. That only creates the potential for the two dogs to confront one another and possibly fight. Keep your focus on your dog, commanding it to walk in step with you and correct it if it fails to obey you or ignore the other dog. A water bomb or Bark Busters training pillow can also be used to fend off an aggressive dog. Drop the water bomb or pillow at the dog's feet to startle it, not to hit it. Some need to be conditioned before they will respond the first time. You can also carry food in a pouch and throw it away from you if a threatening dog approaches.

TERRITORIALISM

Instinct also drives a dog to claim and protect what it considers its territory. Your dog's ancestors would have claimed a territory that provided for their survival, including shelter, access to water, and food. Even though we provide for most of our dog's needs, the territorial instinct is still very strong today. A dog, by nature, will want to protect its territory if a strange person or animal enters. They will also protect their owners the same way they would protect a pack leader in the wild and their owner's possessions, which they see as belonging to the pack.

Typically, a dog will bark to warn the intruder or to call the pack; barking, therefore, is not always a precursor to an attack. But if a dog continues to feel threatened, it is more likely to attack to defend itself.

If your dog is overprotective of you or your property and acting aggressively toward strangers, the best way to correct this problem is through scene setting and conditioning. Ask a friend who is a stranger to the dog to visit your house to help you. Place the dog on a lead with training collar, but leave the lead on the ground rather than holding it in your hand. Instead, plant your foot firmly on the lead. Have a water spray bottle or Bark Busters training pillow in hand to create a diversion when your helper knocks at the door. Use your water spray bottle or drop the pillow on the floor near the dog at the precise moment the dog becomes aggressive, stepping on the lead at the same time. Alternatively, another friend (whom the dog knows and respects) could hold the lead loosely. Then, when the dog becomes aggressive, have your friend check the lead and use the spray bottle or training pillow to correct the dog. This scenario will need to be repeated several times, with different helpers.

MARKING

Dogs will often "mark" their territory by urinating or defecating in strategic areas, similar to how humans might erect a fence or other visible boundary. Marking, to a dog, informs intruders that this area is already claimed. Marking is not only a male trait. Although female dogs usually squat to urinate, some very territorial females will imitate the male and try to cock their legs as high as possible.

To discourage a dog from marking in a particular area, place its drinking water in that spot. As a rule, dogs will avoid marking near where they eat and drink. Inside marking can also be discouraged by spraying citronella on the problem areas.

AGGRESSION CAUSED BY POSSESSIVENESS

A dog can act aggressively if you try to take something away that it is protecting or holds particularly dear. This could be a favorite object, food, even a person. The maternal instinct can also spur a female dog to become more aggressive in order to protect the litter. In the wild, the pups would be prone to attack from other dogs, usually males, that view the new pack members as a potential threat to their position. This behavior may be particularly strong with the birth of a first litter, but in all cases it will diminish as the pups mature.

CASE STUDY

A female poodle owned by a couple had become very attached to the male owner. Whenever she saw the man kiss or cuddle his wife, she would bark at them until they stopped. The couple were in a quandary as to how to fix the problem, so they called Bark Busters.

We told the man to give the dog something pleasant to eat (her favorite treat) the next time he kissed his wife. In this way, the dog would come to associate the kissing and cuddling with a good experience. With repeated effort (and a number of treats), the dog was cured.

KLEPTOMANIA

The dictionary defines kleptomania as "an irresistible urge to steal." But if your dog is a "canine klepto," the dog is not really stealing, not in the true sense of the word. A dog does not have a conscience and does not know it is taking something that does not belong to it. A dog considers itself a member of a pack, and anything in the house is, after all, the pack's possessions.

A dog that takes things is just showing instinctual possessiveness and taking advantage of an opportunity. When it sees something it wants, it merely seizes the object for its own. The "stolen" item can be any item the dog feels it wants to own: a shoe, a bone, your wallet, an article of clothing.

Most dogs will give up their booty relatively easily, and many dog owners look at the behavior with amusement, saying "The placemats are missing again. Check Fido's bed." But if your dog becomes aggressive when you try to retrieve the item, a cure must be implemented.

To control this type of problem, you need to show the dog that you are dominant. Start with the conditioning methods described in Section Three. With your dog on the lead, start to take the object away. Use a water spray bottle or drop a training pillow near the dog and growl BAH at the exact moment it snaps or growls, and pat or voice-praise it when it relents.

CASE STUDY

Cleo was a five-year-old female Old English sheepdog crossbreed. She would snatch things that were either dropped or left lying around and would fiercely repel any attempts by her owners, a family of three, to get their possessions back. She would fly under the bed and snap and growl when anyone tried to reach under the bed.

The owners had tried unsuccessfully for over a year to cure their dog's kleptomania and aggressive behavior. Cleo proved to be a friendly, loving dog, who showed no signs of aggression to us. We decided to check her out by dropping articles and allowing her to take them to her lair under the bed. We were able to calmly retrieve them without any resistance.

Her owners then showed us how they attempted to get their possessions back. They would thrust their hands under the bed but withdraw them quickly when the dog would growl or snap. Their apprehension made the dog think she had the upper hand.

We prescribed a week of programming and conditioning before attempting treatment. Then we suggested that the owners place her on a Bark Busters training collar and strong webbing lead. Although they had conditioned their dog, the lead would assist them if they met any further resistance and enable them to restrain the dog if it launched an attack.

It took only a little discipline to cure Cleo's kleptomania.

OVERPROTECTIVE OF PEOPLE

Because dogs depend upon the pack for survival, they are naturally protective of the other pack members. When a dog is overly possessive of a person, that person must be the one to correct the dog. This is one of the few times we recommend using food for training purposes.

FOOD PROTECTION AND AGGRESSION

Dogs, by instinct, are possessive of their food. A dog in the wild would have stiff competition for food from other pack members and would guard it very carefully. Survival in the wild depended on it. The instincts of dogs, both wild and domesticated, are designed for self-preservation, and a dog will naturally drive off any person or animal that might try to take its food away. Owners can have trouble understanding this; after all, they are the ones who feed their dogs. But remember, dogs cannot reason and are governed by instinct unless trained to act otherwise.

A dog that does not allow you near it while it is eating must be corrected. A dog could attack not only while it is eating its regular food, but also if children were to come too close to a spot where it has buried a bone. For this reason, a dog with food-aggression problems should not be given a bone until the problem is corrected.

Food aggression can be a serious and potentially dangerous problem. You should seek professional help if you have an older dog exhibiting this kind of behavior or a puppy that is not successfully corrected by using the following techniques.

A good conditioning technique for a puppy is to make it sit every time you approach to feed it. You may need to put a lead on the dog to ensure you have enough control. Holding the lead, place the food on the ground, and wait about thirty seconds. If your pup starts to move toward the food, say BAH in a deep, growling tone, stepping on the lead at the same time. It's best if your puppy remains in a seated position but not critical as long as it does not rush for the food. Always release the pressure on the lead and praise your puppy as soon as it stops going for the food. Once you are satisfied that your puppy understands what you want and is waiting for permission from you, say FREE and encourage it to eat. Praise it, saying "Good dog" as it does.

Be sure to follow the same ritual every time you feed your puppy to reinforce the correct behavior. Inconsistency on your part will only confuse your puppy, whereas consistency will reassure the puppy that you are a good leader and will meet its need for an ordered life.

Puppies displaying food aggression can also be corrected by scattering their food on the floor, instead of using a food bowl. Many puppies learn to associate the feeding dish with the need to protect their food from a young age, usually when they were first weaned and were forced to fight other puppies over food in the bowl. Without the food bowl, they have nothing to protect.

Another method that works well is hand-feeding, especially if you are using raw meaty bones. Just keep the food bowl on the kitchen counter, out of reach of the puppy. Feed the puppy one piece at a time, always waiting for it to finish the first before handing it the next piece.

PREDATORY AGGRESSION

The hunting instinct is basic to the wild dog's survival. A domesticated dog that displays predatory aggression by going after a pet rabbit or cat has not turned savage; it is only acting naturally. Like other forms of aggression, predatory attacks can be controlled with good training.

There is also no basis to the belief that once a dog has "tasted blood," it will attack relentlessly. A wild dog did not attack the members of its pack when it returned from the hunt. Feeding a dog raw meat or bones does not make it more likely to attack.

As with other behavioral problems, prevention is the best defense. Always place a young dog on a lead when it is around other animals and teach it to respect you and follow your commands from an early age. As the dog's owner, you need to show strong disapproval of any predatory behavior. To do so, you may need to use one of the recommended training aids (see Section Three for more information on the use of training aids) to distract the dog, growling BAH at the same time, and then praising the dog as soon as it stops misbehaving. You will probably have to repeat these actions several times before your dog learns to ignore other animals. A muzzle may be necessary for a dog that is very difficult to handle.

TRAINED AGGRESSION

Sometimes, aggressive behavior is the result of the actions of a dog's owner or other humans with whom it has come in contact. A dog may have become aggressive because the owner mistakenly tried to pat and soothe it when it began acting aggressively. Such actions by the owner only increase the dog's aggression because it feels it is being praised for its behavior.

In response to an increasing crime rate, some owners have intentionally had their dogs professionally trained to be aggressive toward strangers and more protective of the owners' property. A dog that is trained to be aggressive has simply had its natural protective instincts finely tuned and strengthened.

This type of dog could be dangerous in the wrong hands; it could become suspicious of everyone and act aggressively toward anyone it encounters. Since dogs have neither a conscience nor the ability to reason, the owner needs to be in full control at all times. Whatever the origins of your dog's trained aggression, you can control it by conditioning it to the correction techniques outlined in Section Three.

Aggressive Behavior Caused by Visitors

Some aggression can be traced to negative memories of rough or otherwise thoughtless treatment by visitors. Overexuberance problems can arise when visitors play games that encourage the puppy to act out. Some guests will want to play rough hand games with a puppy. This only creates future handling problems because the puppy will believe that all hands are for biting each time a human hand comes near it. Discourage your guests from playing rough games with your puppy.

CASE STUDY

Bark Busters was called to treat Regal, a shy Scottish collie, for excessive barking caused by a fear of strangers. The dog's fear had arisen from two traumatic experiences when she was a young, impressionable puppy of about three months of age.

The first trauma occurred when a friend of the owner picked the puppy up and literally threw her across the room to someone else. A short time later, another friend came to visit. When he entered, Regal began barking. The visitor chased the puppy through the house, imitating the way she was barking. Eventually, poor Regal was a shivering wreck in the corner, wetting herself with fright.

As a result of these two experiences, Regal became very shy around strangers and would bark frantically at them, hoping they would run away and leave her alone.

We prescribed conditioning for about a week, followed by some "stranger desensitization. "This involved having strangers visit the house on a regular basis to rebuild the dog's confidence around visitors. We stressed that Regal's owner would have to be very selective in her choice of friends to help rehabilitate her dog.

We also asked Regal's owner to correct the dog each time she barked, using the Bark Busters training pillow. She was instructed to drop it on the ground near the dog's back legs and growl BAH, and then to praise the dog with vigorous patting as soon as she stopped misbehaving. A strong correction was necessary in this case in order to change Regal's habits. If a shy dog has a barking problem, fear can be difficult, but not impossible, to overcome.

Physical Causes of Aggression

There are a number of medical or physical conditions that can cause aggressive behavior. Some medications alter a dog's brain chemistry, and when discontinued, the dog may experience withdrawal symptoms. Disease can also cause dramatic personality changes. Distemper, which attacks the brain, can actually make a dog hallucinate. Rabies and brain tumors also alter how a dog behaves.

Sexual Aggression

Hormones can have a significant impact on behavior. The male hormone may be one reason why male dogs are often more playful than female dogs. In the wild, this trait created opportunities for young dogs to try out sexual advances and physical confrontations with other dogs in the pack to establish their hierarchical position.

More serious aggression and destructive behavior can occur when a female dog is in season. As discussed in Section Two, an otherwise well-behaved but unspayed female can suddenly become disobedient, while male dogs can be quite destructive and aggressive when pursuing a female in heat. This is an important reason for neutering your dog.

CASE STUDY

Tyson was an eight-month-old German shepherd. His sexual indiscretions were proving difficult: he was constantly riding the legs of his owners and their guests.

When we met Tyson, he proceeded to do the same to us. His owners said, "Feel privileged; he likes you." But we could see that Tyson's sexual advances were his way of controlling and dominating people. Unfortunately, no one had been willing to correct him.

Our first objective was to establish a rapport with the dog by offering him doggy treats. Then, accompanied by the owner, we took Tyson for a walk around the block to make sure he responded to our instructions.

When we returned from the walk, we showed the owners how to program and condition Tyson to the BAH word. We told his owners to continue conditioning Tyson for five minutes each day. They should use the BAH word each time he tried his sexual advances, and then give him a doggy treat immediately when he ceased.

It took Tyson's owners only two weeks of repeated training to cure his problem completely.

BARKING

While aggressive dogs may bark, a barking dog is not necessarily aggressive. Dogs would bark in the wild primarily to warn other members of the pack about an impending threat. Similarly, the domesticated dog barks to alert its owner. This is one of the reasons why dogs and people began living together. Prehistoric people soon realized the benefits of having a creature around that could warn them of approaching danger.

Unfortunately, in a society where people live in close proximity, a barking dog can be more of a hindrance than a help. A good guard dog will let you know when a stranger is entering your property, not when they are several blocks away or even walking past your house. Dogs shouldn't bark at other dogs, birds, cats, squirrels, or the neighbors.

What dogs bark at depends on their breed and temperament. Some timid dogs will bark at anything that moves. Herding dogs, such as collies, Welsh corgis, and Australian cattle dogs, will usually bark at and attack anything with wheels, such as lawn mowers, motorcycles, cars, and skateboards. Terriers usually bark at people and other dogs, as do Dobermans, German shepherds and Rottweilers. The hunting and sporting breeds are more prone than others to howling or barking when left alone. This group includes the Labradors, retrievers, pointers and spaniels.

Even the most vociferous barkers can be trained to change their habits. To cure your dog of excessive barking, you need to catch it in the act. Sneak up and throw a water bomb or Bark Busters training pillow on the ground near the dog's feet or bounce one of them against a fence or tin shed, while you say BAH. Praise your dog the instant it stops barking.

CASE STUDY

A German shepherd named Zoe barked frequently, which had caused her owners to lose numerous friendships and hours of sleep. The local council had also threatened action. Her owners tried tranquilizers as a temporary solution, but the medication only knocked the dog out, which was equally distressing. Next, they bought a sonic collar that emitted a high-pitched sound every time the dog barked. Zoe, being a highly intelligent dog, learned to bark in tune with the sound of the collar.

When we were called to help, we began by teaching the owner how to condition and program Zoe to the BAH word. Then, we set the scene to get her to bark by having a friend walk past the house with her dog.

When Zoe ran barking at the dog and its owner, we instructed Zoe's owners to correct her by lobbing the training pillow at the fence in front of her. Zoe responded.

We instructed the owners to continue the treatment with similar scene setting. Within two weeks, Zoe was cured. Since then, she has learned to bark only at people who enter the property unannounced.

You can even train your dog to bark at specific things or circumstances and not at others. But first you must train yourself to respond accordingly, by correcting or praising your dog's barking. Teaching the dog how to differentiate between good and bad barking will take time and effort, but it can be done as long as you are persistent.

Puppies and Barking

You should expect some barking the first few nights after you bring a new puppy home, but a well-adjusted and well-bred puppy will rarely bark once it is settled in its new home. Excessive barking in a young pup could be an indication of an undesirable temperament and should be corrected immediately using the BAH correction word. Most puppies will respond well to the techniques in the Sliding Scale of Correction, as outlined in Section Three, unless they are barking out of fear. In those cases, what they are afraid of, which could just be the unknown, may supersede their fear of being disciplined. (For more information on puppies and barking, see Section Two.)

Barking at Night

Dogs are generally more protective at night, the time when a pack in the wild would be most vulnerable. Dogs are also generally more alert at night, when we are sleeping. The cure for night barking depends on where your dog sleeps. If it is your bedroom, then it will be easier to correct your dog. Simply keep a water sprayer handy or a training pillow by your bedside and drop one of them while saying BAH when your dog barks. But if your dog sleeps in another room in the house or outside, you will need to put in a little extra effort.

To cure a dog that barks in the backyard at night, open a window near where the dog usually is when it barks. Have some corrective missiles ready, either a couple of water bombs or a training pillow. As soon as your dog starts barking, land them close to the dog or bounce them off a fence or wall. Remember to growl BAH when you throw one of the corrective training aids and praise your dog when it stops barking. More persistent dogs may require you to go to the dog to correct it, using the same techniques.

Once your dog is conditioned to the corrective technique you have selected, you can correct your dog without getting out of bed as long as your dog is within earshot. Simply set up a metal receptacle, such as a cooking pot or colander, near your bed. Then, if your dog starts barking, you can simply toss the training pillow into the receptacle, which will amplify the sound so that the dog can hear it. Praise your dog with your voice when it stops barking.

Barking Out the Window

A dog that starts barking inside the house whenever it spots someone or something walking by, such as a cat or another dog, can be bothersome and quite nerve-wracking. If you live in close proximity to others, this could cause problems for you and your neighbors. Apartment dwellers have often been forced to move if they cannot control their dogs' barking.

When you catch your dog barking, use your water spray bottle or Bark Busters training pillow and the BAH word to correct it, followed by praise when it stops barking. A particularly quick cure can be achieved with some scene setting. Ask a friend to walk past your house, possibly with another dog on lead. Then, correct your dog in the same way as before when it starts barking. Do this several times until your dog stops barking at passersby. Keep the water spray bottle or training pillow nearby to handle future outbreaks.

Barking at Neighbors

If your dog barks at your neighbors, ask them to help you correct the problem. While you observe from a window, ask your neighbors to walk into their yard in the dog's line of sight. Then, when your dog starts barking, throw one of the training aids at a fence or near the dog's feet and growl BAH. Once you start the training session, you must continue until the dog's barking has been cured.

You can also perform this exercise from your neighbor's yard. Pretend to go out and hide in their yard, from a spot where you are out of the dog's sight but can lob the necessary corrective aids the moment your dog barks. If your dog is not aggressive toward strangers, you can eventually ask your neighbors to correct it while you are out.

If you are not on good terms with your neighbors, you will have to correct the problem yourself. Just wait for your dog to bark at your neighbors, then correct it as described above. Be patient; it may take longer, since you will need to wait until the dog misbehaves rather than being able to create the situation yourself.

Barking at Guests

Dogs that bark at guests usually have a nervous disposition or conversely are very dominant. If yours is the nervous type, set the scene to correct its behavior. Ask a neighbor or friend to visit. Keep your dog on its lead, and as soon as it starts barking, use your water spray bottle or Bark Busters training pillow and say BAH. It can be difficult to get a nervous dog to stop barking, as sometimes they are more nervous than they are respectful of the correction. But keep at it; nervous dogs are hard, but not impossible, to train, as long as you remain strong and persistent.

Repeat the procedure several times with different friends coming to the door. You need to desensitize the dog to other people. A nervous dog may never be friendly toward others or let them pet it, but it can learn to tolerate them without barking. Ask future guests not to pet your dog and to otherwise ignore it, which will help calm your dog down. Confronting a nervous dog only puts pressure on it and can cause unnecessary stress.

You need to employ a different technique if your dog is more dominant. Ask for help from two people whom your dog knows and respects, such as family members. Keep your dog on its lead, and ask one person to act like a visitor and the other to hide behind the other person. When the person knocks and you open the door, the person hiding should come into view and correct the dog with the BAH word in the most dominant voice he or she can muster, while throwing your chosen corrective training aid at the dog's feet as soon as it starts barking.

If your dog fails to respond fully, escalate the level of correction. This time, both you and a helper should hide behind the friend who knocks on the door. Then, when your dog starts barking, both of you should come out of hiding and use one or more of the training aids while growling BAH to correct the dog. Repeat this procedure until your dog stops barking; then praise it.

Do not try these exercises off lead until you are very confident the dog will not return to its old behavior. You will need to condition your dog with the help of different friends; otherwise, the dog will only behave correctly around the person(s) with whom the training was conducted.

Barking or Jumping at the Back Door

To cure a dog of barking behind a closed door, wait until it barks and then instantly open the door and drop a water bomb or Bark Busters training pillow at the floor near the dog's feet while saying BAH. Repeat this procedure until the dog stops barking, and then praise it for behaving.

The water spray bottle is an effective training tool for a dog that jumps at the screen door or barks through it. As soon as your dog barks or jumps, spray water at it through the screen. Dogs that jump up on sliding glass doors can be cured by throwing the training pillow at the metallic base. But be careful not to hit the glass; you could break it. As soon as the dog stops misbehaving, let it know you are pleased by praising it.

Barking When You are Out

To stop a dog from barking when you are out, you have to do some scene setting. Pretend to go out, then sneak back and hide while a friend walks a dog past your house. As soon as your dog barks, jump out and correct it by growling BAH and using one of the training aids. Set a similar scene but with different people and animals, so that your dog does not think it will only be corrected when that particular person and/or animal walks by.

Barking When a Car Comes or Goes from Your Driveway

You need to do some more scene setting for this one. Ask a friend to drive in and out of your driveway. Hide nearby (as close as you can to your dog without it seeing you). When your dog starts barking, immediately use one of the selected training aids and growl BAH. Praise the dog when it responds.

Barking while Penned or Chained

Penning a dog is more humane than chaining one, although we recognize there are times when an owner has no other choice. If you do chain your dog, use a running chain, if possible, as described on page 53, and make sure you take your dog for walks and exercise it often. Water bombs or a Bark Busters training pillow can be used to cure dogs that bark while penned or chained. Just bounce one of them off the kennel while growling BAH. Praise the dog when it stops barking.

Barking at the Vacuum Cleaner

A vacuum cleaner can be a very scary looking contraption to a dog that has no understanding of what it is or why it makes the sound that it does. Fortunately, it is easy to stop a dog from barking at it. Keep a water spray bottle or training pillow handy; then use one of them in conjunction with the BAH word when the dog starts barking. You can even do this if your dog starts barking when you go to the closet or wherever you keep the vacuum. Be prepared every time you get ready to vacuum, and always praise your dog when it stops barking. You can use the same corrective technique if your dog barks at a broom or other similar cleaning device.

Barking at Your Commands

If a dog does not respect you, it will likely bark back at your commands, much like a teenager who talks back to his or her parents. Do not condone this behavior. Correct your dog repeatedly with the BAH word in conjunction with the water sprayer or Bark Busters training pillow until you are successful. Then praise the dog for responding to your commands. This problem can usually be cured relatively quickly.

Barking While You Are in the Pool

If you have a pool and a dog that tends to bark whenever you are in it, you will need help to cure this problem. Not only are you lower in height than your dog, which is a less dominant position, but splashing water can also excite the dog.

Have a family member go swimming while you hide nearby. When your dog starts to bark, jump out and use one of the training tools while correcting it with the BAH word. You may have to do this a few times before your dog stops barking, but when it does, remember to praise it. Once you have conditioned your dog in this manner, you should have better luck correcting it, if necessary, from the pool yourself.

DESTRUCTIVE CHEWING AND DIGGING

Just about everyone expects puppies to chew, but many adult dogs will continue to chew or exhibit other destructive behavior, such as digging. From our experience, there is a connection between a dog's intelligence and its destructive behavior. A high percentage of the dogs we have been asked to treat for this problem have proven to be very intelligent animals. Of course, there are other factors that promote destructive behavior, such as boredom, stress, lack of adequate housing, and lack of purpose, as well as a diet high in carbohydrates, colorings, and/or preservatives. However, we have seen dogs of lower intelligence forced to live under these conditions that have not exhibited destructive behavior.

CASE STUDY

Klint was a two-year-old German shepherd with a destructive chewing problem. His owner was reluctantly searching for a new owner for Klint because the dog's behavior was getting expensive. Most recently, the dog had destroyed the entire interior of his owner's brand-new Volvo. Other than chewing and digging, the owner said Klint was usually very well behaved and did not bark. As such, he had not thought training was necessary.

After meeting Klint and his owner, we were convinced that the dog's problem was a lack of mental stimulation. Klint was far too intelligent to go through life without any outlet for his intellect. He chewed because he was bored. Klint needed to be active, and training could provide a much-needed challenge.

We showed the owner how to condition Klint to the BAH word and set a daily regimen that was tailored to the owner's busy schedule. This consisted of a twenty-minute training procedure that included assorted obedience exercises, such as teaching the dog to sit, stay, and drop/stay. The owner was also instructed to take Klint on a disciplined walk every day. By disciplined, we meant that the dog should learn to walk at the owner's pace without stopping to sniff trees or investigate other distractions. We wanted Klint to use his brain, rather than just ambling.

We also suggested that the owner erect a secure pen for Klint, which would help prevent the dog from destroying anything else of value before the treatment was complete. The cost of the pen would soon be offset by the absence of destructive chewing. We also recommended a Buster Cube to keep Klint mentally occupied.

Four weeks after treatment commenced, we heard that the pen had stopped Klint's destructiveness immediately. The dog was now able to leave the pen and no longer chewed. Thanks to the training and the Buster Cube, Klint was a much happier dog.

There are also some breeds of dogs that are more prone to chewing and digging than others. Many larger breeds, such as collies, Labradors, and German shepherds, are likely to have such problems. Australian cattle dogs, poodles, and terriers head the list for the smaller dogs.

PUPPIES AND CHEWING

It's difficult to stop a puppy from chewing, as it needs to bite on something firm while teething, much like a baby does. The easiest method is simply to keep your puppy away from things you don't want it to chew. Put your pup in a playpen with items you don't mind it chewing, such as bones, teething biscuits (the same as used for infants) or chew toys. If you use a toy, make sure it is not made of a brittle material that could break off and lodge in the puppy's mouth or stomach.

When your puppy is out of its playpen, pick up everything that you do not want destroyed, such as shoes and children's toys, and put them away until the dog is older. You cannot expect a puppy to know what it can and cannot touch, and it will be drawn to just about everything, especially items with its owner's scent on them.

STRESS

A dog that constantly chews, howls, or digs could be a stressed dog. This stress may arise if the dog is left alone at home. In a pack situation, a dog would almost always accompany the rest of the pack when they went hunting. So, it stands to reason that, when we leave our dogs alone, they don't understand why they cannot accompany the other members of the pack; in this case, their owners.

Hormone imbalances can also cause the dog to chew as a result of stress. If you suspect this may be the cause, talk to your vet to see if your dog has hormone imbalances or whether neutering or spaying would be helpful.

CASE STUDY

Danny's German shepherd, Cinta, was very well behaved and rarely chewed, until the time Danny went to the hospital for a week. Upon his return, he immediately went out to greet the dog who was delighted to see him. Unfortunately, Danny had to leave again on business. When he returned home three hours later, Cinta had demolished the wooden veranda, chewing every bit of railing she could find. The stress of seeing her beloved owner only for a few seconds after he had been away for so long and then to have him leave again upset her too much.

If you are gone a lot, the ideal situation is to have two dogs that can keep each other company. A male and female that are neutered and spayed, respectively, make ideal companions. Same sex dogs are more prone to fighting. A puppy and a kitten option also work well. But if you prefer just one dog, there is another way to cure your dog's stress from being left alone. Just like other problems, to be successful, you must catch your dog in the act of chewing and correct it immediately.

Once your dog is conditioned to the BAH word as a correction, you can pretend to leave by going somewhere out of the dog's sight and wait for it to start chewing. By coming out of hiding while the dog is chewing and using the BAH correction, along with a water spray bottle or training pillow if necessary, you can make the dog think you are always there and reduce the stress it feels when alone. As an added precaution, you can also protect your belongings by applying something with an unpleasant taste, such as Bitter Apple®, which can be purchased at your local pet store or from your local Bark Busters therapist. There are several other safe dog repellants on the market as well. Ask your veterinarian or local pet store for suggestions.

DIGGING

Dogs are natural diggers. In the wild, they would dig burrows to provide protection from heat and cold, while a pregnant female would dig a lair in which to give birth to her puppies and protect them. Dogs also dig to bury food and preserve it for later.

Over-feeding your dog or giving it large bones can also trigger the instinct to dig, as can a lack of proper nutrients. Many dogs will dig in search of minerals and vegetation that are lacking in their diet. If digging is a problem, your dog may benefit from raw vegetables or a mineral supplement. Make sure these issues are not causing your dog to dig before trying out the other corrective measures outlined below.

Most importantly, keep in mind that if your dog is digging, even if it is in your favorite garden, it is quite normal behavior, but it can still be corrected.

Many ardent gardeners have asked us, puzzled, why their dogs continue to re-dig holes that the owners just refilled. Ask yourself this question: if you dug a hole and then went to a nursery to buy a tree to plant, only to come home and find the hole filled, what would you do? Most likely, you would dig the hole again. Your dog will do the same.

Like chewing, catching your dog in the act can be tricky. Deliberately bury some food; then hide and wait for your dog to start digging it up. At that precise moment it does, you can growl BAH and use your chosen corrective training aid. If catching your dog in the act proves too challenging, here are a few more suggestions:

1. After filling a hole your dog has dug, place some of the dog's drop-pings on top. That should be an effective deterrent.
2. Another method is to place some hot chili powder in each hole your dog has dug. Be sure to let him smell the powder on your hands so that it remembers the unpleasant smell. (Note that dogs have a stronger sense of smell than taste and do not need to actually taste the powder.)

These two methods will stop your dog from digging in places you have effec-tively booby-trapped, but they will not stop your dog from digging elsewhere. The best advice is to try the last two techniques for preventative purposes, but continue to try to catch your dog in the act and correct it.

PUPPIES AND DIGGING

As with the problem of chewing, playpens can physically restrict a puppy from digging. As an alternative, you can create a sandpit where your puppy can dig to its heart's content. As an added benefit, your puppy will be able to dig to find shade and shelter from extreme heat or cold. Create a sandpit in a child's durable wading pool and place it near a weatherproof kennel and close to the house to further ward off stress. Remember, puppies and dogs like to be close to home.

BITING

Since dogs do not have hands, they use their mouths for just about everything. Biting is usually more prominent in a dominant puppy or dog or one that per-ceives you as weaker than it is. Licking, on the other hand, is primarily exhib-ited by a more submissive dog.

Hand biting can stem from someone in the family playing roughly with your puppy. Young children and adolescents are the greatest offenders. They tend to want to rough up the puppy and will thrust their hands toward it, playing a game that incites biting. If you follow the rule that "hands are for petting only," you will have fewer problems with hand biting. However, if you have a puppy or dog that bites your hands, try the following steps:

1. When your dog appears ready to bite your hand, freeze and growl BAH. Do not pull your hand away; pulling back will only encourage the puppy to persist. If properly conditioned, your dog should stop and look at you. If it responds as it should, praise it. Then try to pet your dog. If it tries to bite your hand again, repeat the above process. If you have a more determined puppy that refuses to stop regardless of how much you growl, escalate to Step Two.

2. Fill a spray bottle with water. Keep it hidden behind your back and pet your dog. If it tries to bite your hand, freeze, and using your other hand, squirt the puppy just under the chin, while growling BAH. Again, praise the puppy when it stops biting. Squirt and growl BAH if it starts to bite again. Remember to freeze the actions of the hand that is about to be bitten and to squirt with the other hand. This will usually discourage the most determined puppy, but you must be consistent. The reason for growling BAH is to condition your puppy to react to the vocal correction alone.

3. Finally, if all else fails, escalate the correction to include a Bark Busters training pillow.

To assist in the process, you can smear your hands with mustard to make your dog associate your hand with an unpleasant taste.

If your dog bites your ankles or clothing, immediately escalate the corrective technique to include use of one of the training aids discussed in Section

Three. Wait for your dog to grab your clothing or ankles. Then, while you stand still, employ the training aid and growl BAH. Praise your dog, saying "Good boy" or "Good girl" the instant it stops biting.

JUMPING UP ON PEOPLE

Jumping up is one of the most common problems and one of the easiest to solve. The problem usually starts when the dog is a puppy. Dog owners and visitors often make the mistake of encouraging a puppy to jump up when it is little because they prefer not to have to bend down to pet it. From then on, the dog thinks that this is what it should do if it wants a pat, even when it is fully grown.

Puppies in the wild would also jump up, usually to encourage their mother or other members of the pack to regurgitate food they might have brought back from the hunt. Later in their development, puppies use jumping to test their opponents' dominance in playing and fighting. Jumping is a dog's way of asserting its dominance over dogs and members of its pack, including humans.

Start by conditioning the dog to respond to the BAH word. Then when it jumps up, freeze, just as a dominant dog in the wild would do. Most people respond by trying to push the dog back down, a natural defensive reaction for humans, but not for dogs. They will think you want to play and wrestle.

For some dogs, this is all it will take. But other dogs are more determined, and you will need to escalate the correction according to the sliding scale of correction, as explained in Section Three.

Try clapping your hands, spraying your dog with water or dropping one of the training aids as you say BAH. Praise your dog the instant it has all four feet on the ground. Repeat the process until the dog stops jumping up. You will eventually gain control by just freezing your actions and growling BAH.

Teach all other adult family members to do the same, and jumping will soon become a problem of the past.

If your dog jumps on guests, you can either instruct them how to respond or you can set a scene with some friends; be prepared to use one of the training aids when the dog starts to jump up.

This technique will not work, however, if your dog tries to jump up on young children. Dogs will generally not respect children nor accept a correction from them. (See more on dogs and children in Section Six.) For this reason, you will need to set up situations where a dog tries to jump up on children. Have the children

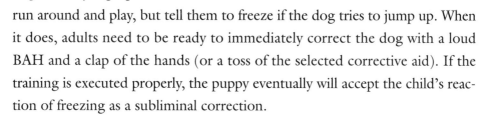

run around and play, but tell them to freeze if the dog tries to jump up. When it does, adults need to be ready to immediately correct the dog with a loud BAH and a clap of the hands (or a toss of the selected corrective aid). If the training is executed properly, the puppy eventually will accept the child's reaction of freezing as a subliminal correction.

JUMPING OVER THE FENCE

Dogs usually learn at a young age how to jump a fence and escape confinement. Unfortunately, once a dog has gained its freedom, it will continue to try to escape, even if you have secured the area. For this reason, the best cure is prevention by making sure your puppy or dog cannot escape beginning with the first day it comes home with you.

If your dog has already learned how to jump a fence, scene setting can help. Pretend to leave your property and hide out of the dog's sight, but in a place where you can still see it. Wait for the dog to try to escape, and when it does, use one of the corrective training aids and growl BAH.

JUMPING ON FURNITURE

A lot of new puppy owners will allow their dogs to sleep with them. We know one woman who now sleeps with a full-grown Great Dane because she let it do so when it was a pup. You can't expect a dog to "grow out" of wanting to sleep on a bed once it has become accustomed to it.

Dogs will often sneak onto furniture, such as a bed or couch, while you are out or otherwise preoccupied in another room. It's an easy problem to cure, but you will need to set the scene. Hide in a closet or under or behind the bed. Arm yourself with a water sprayer or training pillow, and be prepared to wait. If your dog only jumps on the furniture when it thinks you are gone, it could be awhile before it is convinced you are not there. But once it does enter the room and starts to jump on the bed or other furniture, suddenly appear from your hiding spot and use the spray bottle or drop the training pillow while growling BAH. Praise your dog when it jumps down.

There is an easier way to solve this problem. Simply block access to rooms and furniture off limits to your dog.

RUSHING THROUGH A DOOR OR GATE

We have already discussed how to condition your dog not to rush through a gate before you without your permission under Conditioning in Section Three. As a reminder, put your dog on lead with a training collar and start walking your dog toward the gate or door. Check your dog with a snap of the lead and collar and growl BAH if it tries to pull ahead or go through the gate. Then, have your dog sit at a spot just before the gate; open it and go through the gate yourself. Correct the dog if it moves from its position before you say FREE.

TRAVELING IN THE CAR

Although many dogs love traveling in the car, there are dogs that find it extremely traumatic. To those dogs, the car is a very strange environment. Not only is the motion of the vehicle unsettling, but the space inside the car is also compact and enclosed. In such a situation, a dog can feel threatened or cornered because it appears as if there is no way out. Some dogs may become excited in the car and bark constantly. Others may run from one side of the car to the other. Be prepared for these possibilities when you take your dog in the car for the first time, and insist on good manners from the outset. If you let a dog jump or bark, it will think it's okay to always behave this way.

As with most other situations, it is best to get your dog used to the car as early as possible in its life. Try sitting with your dog in the car, just parked in the driveway with the doors open. Try it next time with the doors shut, then with the engine on. After that, attempt a short trip around the block. Soon your dog should understand that it has nothing to fear.

The most effective way to travel with a dog is to tie it with a lead, either to the arm rest or to the seat belt anchor. There are also doggy safety harnesses that prevent the dog from jumping all over the car.

To stop a dog from barking while you are traveling, you can try spraying it with a water bottle or dropping a Bark Busters training pillow into a wok or small pot on the car floor. The pot will amplify the sound of the training pillow and create an immediate diversion from what it was doing; coupled with the BAH correction word, this should stop even the most chronic barkers.

GETTING IN AND OUT OF THE CAR

Teaching your dog how to get in and out of a car under your control will be very important if you plan to travel with your dog. A dog that jumps into a car without waiting for its owner's permission can be a nuisance. Imagine your dog covered in mud bounding into your car before you can stop it.

To teach your dog good traveling manners, you will need to position your dog beside your vehicle with its training collar and lead on. The goal is to teach your dog to wait for the FREE command before it gets into or out of the vehicle. With your dog on lead, open the door, using the correction word BAH if it tries to jump in. Check your dog at the same time, tightening and releasing the lead in quick succession, always ending with a slack lead. Then make your dog sit and wait. If it begins to forge ahead but stops, even momentarily, when you check it and give the BAH correction, be sure to praise it immediately in a pleasant voice. After a couple of minutes, say FREE and encourage the dog toward the open door. Praise it as soon as it moves forward. Also give your dog a quick pat or two as it continues to move in the right direction.

Repeat the same exercise when you are getting the dog out of the vehicle, with one difference: this time block the open door with your body. Correct with the BAH word as soon as your dog attempts to jump out. Repeat this exercise several times, and always follow the same procedure every time you open the door.

If you have a dog that panics when you leave it in the car, just hop out of the car for a few moments each time you stop, and then jump back in. Your dog will start getting used to your leaving and being reassured that you will return shortly.

Fear of Traffic

When walking in public, some dogs become very fearful of the loud sounds and great rush of vehicle traffic. Ideally, a puppy should be desensitized at an early age to all kinds of strange environments, including the hustle and bustle of traffic. A pup is best able to cope with change at its young age, but older dogs can still be trained.

You can use the same method that police use to train their horses. It is a process of desensitization through complete saturation in the environment. Sit at a busy intersection with your dog on a good, secure lead and training collar, correcting bad behavior and praising good behavior. Sooner or later the dog will get bored and ignore the passing traffic.

If your dog is one that barks aggressively at traffic, you can cure this, too. Some dogs require only a quick checking of the training collar. Others will need you to use a water bomb or training pillow to reinforce the correction by creating a distraction as you growl BAH. Of course, the dog should be praised the moment it responds.

CHASING CARS

We've already discussed in Section One why dogs continue to chase cars, even after a bad experience. To the dog, it always wins the game because the vehicle drives off in the end. It was able to ward off an intruder. Unfortunately, this habit can be dangerous for both your dog and the drivers.

To stop a dog from chasing cars and motorcycles, you will need help from a couple of friends and a bucket filled with water bombs. Find an empty parking lot and begin by walking your dog around the lot. Ask one friend to drive a car past you while you let the dog off the lead. As soon as your dog begins

to chase the car, toss your water bombs and growl BAH. In this way, you can correct your dog when it is in full chase.

You can also try this technique with a training pillow, but sometimes the sound of the car motor will drown out the sound.

Repeat this technique with several different cars or vehicles, so that the dog understands this correction relates to all passing cars, not just the vehicle used in training.

Chasing anything that moves

It is a very natural thing for a dog to chase anything that moves. This strong instinct is probably what made the dog's ancestors first realize that they could catch their own food. In other words, this instinct is clearly driven by the need to survive.

Although chasing is instinctive, a dog can be trained not to chase. It is better to correct this problem at an early age, preferably in the first twelve months of its life, when the dog has not yet established strong behavioral patterns. For us, training a puppy not to chase begins the first week we bring it home. We introduce it to our other dogs and pets and teach the newcomer to respect them. We then take the pup with us when we go out and attach a long lightweight lead to correct any early chasing. We simply tug on the lead and growl BAH any time the pup shows too much interest in any other animals, vehicles, or bicycles. We also find a deserted field or street and have a friend drive a car and then ride a bicycle up and down past the pup. Again, we correct any undesirable behavior each time the dog runs at the vehicle or bicycle. It may take three to four weeks of long-lead training before you can trust the dog not to chase off the lead.

Solving this problem is slightly more difficult with the older dog that has probably been enjoying the chase for some time. In these cases, owners will need a very firm approach. First, condition your dog to respond to the BAH correction; then attach a very long, lightweight lead without the dog realizing it's on lead and set the scene. Take the dog to a place where it is likely to find something to chase. Stay well hidden, armed with your selected corrective training aid. When the dog begins the chase, jump out from your hiding place and drop the water bomb or training pillow in its path while growling BAH. When the dog responds and stops the chase, praise it lavishly. You will probably have to set this scene several times with other things the dog likes to chase; eventually it will learn to stop simply by hearing the BAH word.

CASE STUDY

Dougal, a five-year-old border collie, had been a chronic chaser since puppyhood. When we met him, he was frantically running after the chickens in a coop. When his owner managed to stop him, he went after a cat instead, and then a car.

To treat Dougal, we first conditioned and programmed him to the BAH word; then we handed the owner a couple of training pillows and instructed him to stay well hidden until the dog was almost at the coop. Meanwhile, we attached a long, lightweight lead to Dougal.

Dougal ran happily toward the coop. We gave him lots of rope because we did not want him to know he was on a lead. Just as he ran at the chickens, his owner popped out from behind a tree and dropped the pillow in his path, loudly growling the BAH word. It landed on the ground just in front of Dougal. He stopped in his tracks and ran to his owner for a well-deserved pat. After praising his dog, the owner tried to walk the dog back toward the chickens again, but Dougal flatly refused. The owner repeated the same process when Dougal tried to chase other things including vehicles.

It took a couple of follow-ups by us and continued training by the owner. After that, Dougal never chased another thing.

More Problems with Food

Pestering You at Meal Time

As much as owners like to treat their dogs, feeding them scraps from the dinner table is not a good idea. Not only can the food make the dog sick, but a begging dog can also be a real bother at meal time. Try feeding your dog at the same time you eat your meals. Then, if your dog comes to the table after it is finished to beg for food, correct it with the BAH word and point away from the table, indicating you do not want it nearby.

Stealing Food

Since dogs do not know right from wrong, food left unattended is an open invitation to help themselves. To stop a dog from stealing food, set the scene. Place some food on a kitchen or coffee table within the dog's reach, then hide and wait for the dog to try to take the food. As it does, sneak up behind your dog and growl BAH and use your water spray bottle or training pillow.

Fussy Eaters

Because food is plentiful in the world of today's domestic dog, the dog's natural instinct to find and eat food is not as strong as it was in the wild. The dog's ancestors, on the other hand, had to hunt to survive, living mainly on small rodents, injured or weak grazing animals, berries, or whatever it could scavenge. Wild dogs, given the opportunity, would eat almost anything that came their way.

The dog's ancestors would have loved being able to scratch at the back door or carry their bowls to their owners! Today, when our dogs do this, we simply fill their bowls with food. No wonder we have fussy eaters.

Unfortunately, when faced with this problem, too many owners give the dog whatever it will eat, which can result in the dog not receiving sufficient nutrition. As we mentioned in Section Two, some breeds, such as the Chihuahuas and the Maltese, tend to be more particular about their food. If at any time your dog refuses to eat what it is given, cover the food with plastic wrap and keep it in the fridge; then periodically offer it to your dog until it eats. This may be difficult or seem cruel, but trust that your dog will not starve. You may wish to consult your vet or pet store about a fussy eater.

Getting into the Garbage

Since dogs often get into the garbage while their owners are gone, you will need to set the scene to correct this bad habit. Place your trash can in plain sight of your dog, but cover the garbage with a piece of plastic or newspaper. Press the garbage down so the plastic or newspaper lies flat. Then sprinkle the top of the paper or plastic with cayenne pepper. That will be sure to give the dog an unpleasant experience the next time it raids the trash.

PULLING DOWN LAUNDRY

The best way to get a dog to stop pulling laundry off the line is to let the laundry correct the dog. Select five old pillowcases and sprinkle each with Bitter Apple or some other doggie repellant. Peg them securely on the line within your dog's reach. When the dog pulls at the laundry, it will experience an unpleasant taste that will serve as an immediate correction.

PROPER BEHAVIOR IN THE HOME

A dog should act in a calm manner when inside your home. A dog that bounds around the house, jumping on furniture or knocking things over, can be quite a nuisance.

Teach your dog to move calmly around in the house by putting it on a lead but letting the lead trail on the ground. As soon as the dog starts bounding about the house, grab the end of the lead and give it a quick tug or stand on it, while growling BAH. Make sure you have time to focus on your dog when conducting this training; don't be distracted doing other things, such as cleaning or cooking. When you are confident the dog can be controlled, take it off lead and use a water spray bottle or Bark Busters training pillow to reinforce your BAH command as necessary.

NERVOUSNESS

We mentioned in Section Two that dogs are born with a certain temperament, and a nervous dog can be one of the most challenging to train. A nervous dog may stand shaking and shivering each time it hears a loud noise or is confronted with something it does not understand.

While you can never change its temperament, there are certain things we can do to improve the quality of life for the nervous dog. A daily dose of vitamin B (we recommend three ounces, but it is best to consult your veterinarian) could improve the nervous system, but only if the dog is vitamin B deficient. If it is, you will notice a difference in about three months.

You should also look at your dog's diet. Are there chemicals, such as preservatives, in the dog food? These additives can sometimes be toxic to the dog, causing allergies that can affect its nervous system. There are many good top quality and natural choices of dog food available that contain no harmful additives. Consult your vet or local pet shop for recommendations.

In this chapter, we have covered many of the most common behavioral problems in dogs. By understanding how dogs learn and communicate, you can more easily determine the nature of the problem and use the Bark Busters training techniques to solve many problems on your own. If you are in doubt or would like further consultation, contact a Bark Busters therapist. More information on how to find a local therapist is available at the end of the book.

Advanced Training and Tricks

This section is all about having fun . . . for both you and your dog. Advanced training will give your dog more freedom and teach it skills that will benefit both of you. Your dog will learn exercises and tricks the Aussie way, tricks that require neither the restraints of the lead nor the tedious repetition of tasks. We will explain not only how to teach your dog advanced skills and tricks but also the value. The variety of training exercises presented here will help you and your dog develop a greater understanding of one another and become closer companions.

TEACHING YOUR DOG TO JUMP

Before you can teach your dog how to jump over obstacles, you must ensure that your dog is physically fit and does not have any major hip or shoulder problems. You may want to have your veterinarian give your dog a medical checkup before attempting this exercise.

A dog should also be fully grown before you teach it to jump. Most breeds reach this stage of development around twelve months of age, although some of the larger breeds, such as Great Danes and Newfoundlands, are not fully grown until they are two years old. If in doubt, check with the breeder or your veterinarian.

The more varied the objects you choose for your dog to jump over the better. That way it will not think that it is only allowed to jump over a specific type of obstacle.

The Method

When you start training your dog to jump, use solid obstacles that it cannot go under.

With your dog on a three-foot lead, step over the obstacle yourself, and then command the dog to join you using the command OVER. It is important that you actually step over the obstacle, rather than walk around it, because your dog will try to imitate you. Keep the lead short and position your dog close to the obstacle. Each time the dog completes the exercise correctly and jumps over the obstacle, praise it lavishly; then repeat the process. Conduct this training three to four times a week, and several times each training session, until your dog jumps reliably upon command.

Gradually increase the height of the jump over a period of a few days, but do not exceed the recommended maximum height for your dog's breed. If you are unsure, check with the local breed owners club. You can find a local club by visiting the American Kennel Club website at www.akc.com. A general rule of thumb is the dog should be able to jump its own height at the shoulder.

CASE STUDY

When we were teaching our German shepherd, Monty, to jump, we visited a friend who worked at a nearby office building. When we arrived with Monty, our friend's young child was also there. This mischievous little boy was in the habit of locking every gate or door in sight. When we were not looking, he closed the self-locking door in the office courtyard on poor Monty. The office security guard was the only one who had a key.

We were not able to lift Monty out, and our friend was concerned that she might lose her job if the security guard had to be called. Then we had an idea. What about commanding Monty to jump over the wall? Even though the wall was over six-feet tall, Monty had scaled higher walls without much difficulty.

So, I commanded Monty, "Over!"

Monty just looked at the wall and barked back as if to say, "Are you serious?" I smiled and again commanded, "Over!"

Now Monty began to stare at the wall, clearly thinking, "She is serious." He crouched and sprang at the wall.

"Good boy," I assured him.

Then he clambered and scratched his way to the top of the wall, grabbing with his front paws and pulling himself up. Meanwhile, I continued to encourage him to leap to the ground, breaking his fall with my arms as he did so. He was very happy to be free again.

Although Monty's adventure was not life threatening, his jump training certainly saved the day.

TEACHING YOUR DOG TO BARK ON COMMAND

You might ask yourself why you would want to teach your dog to bark on command, especially if you have spent considerable time correcting a barking problem. First of all, teaching your dog to bark on command will not undo all your hard work. Because dogs learn by association, a trained dog will normally bark only in situations it associates (through training) with the need to bark, rather than just barking indiscriminately. However, if you train your dog to bark on command and it starts barking excessively or at the wrong time, make sure you correct it immediately with the BAH word. Your dog should learn to bark only when you command it.

Teaching your dog this trick can be helpful in situations such as a threatening person entering your property or for television or movie work. Some movie makers require that a dog bark on command for a particular scene. The only way to ensure that it will do so is to train it.

Most dogs will bark at some time in their lives, and some dogs, based on their temperament, are more vocal than others. Certain breeds also bark more than others. These include the collie, Australian cattle dog, Chihuahua, the various terriers, and sheepdogs. Other dogs, including the basenji and some of the wild dog species (such as wolf hybrids), do not bark, although they may howl. Barking in the wild could alert prey or other hunting animals to a dog's position.

The Method

To teach your dog to bark on command, start by creating a situation that usually causes it to bark, or try holding up some food and exciting the dog with your voice. You could also tie the dog's lead to something and then run around or bounce a ball near your dog. If neither of these methods work, keep trying until you find something that does.

As soon as the dog starts to bark (it could even be just a whimper), say BARK or SPEAK. Practice regularly, several times a day, five days a week (but always being careful not to overtire your dog), and keep repeating the command every time your dog barks or makes a sound. Eventually, it will respond by barking when it hears the command word.

Some dogs take longer to learn this trick than others. Puppies usually catch on very quickly, as they are easy to excite to the point of barking. In general, you should be able to teach your dog to bark on command within four to twelve weeks, as long as you train it every day.

TEACHING YOUR DOG TO FETCH (RETRIEVE)

Fetching comes naturally to most dogs, especially those bred specifically for this purpose, such as Labradors and golden retrievers, to name just a couple. These breeds will pick up anything in their mouths and carry it around without too much persistence on your part; it just may take longer to teach them to come and sit in front of you and hold the object until you remove it from their mouths.

Several breeds are not natural retrievers, including the Doberman, German shepherd, Rottweiler, collie, and some of the smaller lapdogs, among others. However, all dogs can be trained to fetch and carry something, as long as you keep the training fun for them.

The Method for a Natural Retriever

If your dog is a natural retriever but lacks the finishing touches, such as those required for competition, or if you just want more control over your dog's actions, follow these instructions. You will not only teach your dog to fetch and deliver an object to you but also to hold it in its mouth until you say the command GIVE.

Whenever you introduce anything remotely regimental to a dog, it typically loses interest. For this reason, you will initially have to separate the two actions of retrieving and holding the object. Start by playing a game in which you throw an object and your dog chases it. The objective of the game is to get the dog to deliver the object it has fetched to you, something a natural retriever will almost always do. If your dog does not return the object, try the training technique below for dogs that are not natural retrievers.

Once your dog is reliably bringing the object to you, teach it to hold the object in its mouth until you command it otherwise. Start off with a soft item that will not hurt its mouth, such as a rolled towel or a soft chew toy. Ensure that the object is not too big and fits in the dog's mouth with ease. Also, be careful not to use too small an object that could present a choking hazard.

Place your dog on lead, and stand on the lead so that it cannot run away. Gently open your dog's mouth and say HOLD as you place the object in its mouth. We use the command HOLD to teach a dog to continue to hold an object it has fetched in its mouth, rather than dropping it at your feet.

To properly place the object in the dog's mouth, position it just behind its fangs and tilt the dog's head back slightly so that it cannot spit the object out. If your dog tries to eject the object, do not use force. Instead, growl the correction word BAH immediately; then praise your dog when it stops trying to get rid of the object.

Initially, just getting your dog to hold the object while you tilt its head back is sufficient. Leave the object in its mouth for only five seconds; then praise your dog as you take the object gently out of its mouth.

Once your dog holds the object successfully and willingly, you can resume the "throw the object" game. This time, as your dog comes toward you with the object in its mouth, say HOLD, and praise it as long as it continues to follow your command. Use only a very soft tone if you need to correct your dog during training; you want your dog to continue to enjoy itself, and too harsh of a vocal command could cause the dog to drop the object.

Eventually, fetching and holding the object will become a single exercise for your dog, and you will be able to phase out using the HOLD command. The next step is to get your dog to assume the SIT position in front of you, holding the object it has fetched in its mouth. To do so, pat your dog when it arrives in front of you; as you do, press gently down on its rump until it sits. With both patience and practice, the command FETCH alone will cause your dog to grab an object, bring it back to you, and then sit in front of you holding the object until it hears the command GIVE. As you say GIVE, gently remove the article from the dog's mouth, and praise your dog when it lets go. Eventually, the dog will learn to release an object when it hears the GIVE command.

Even if your dog already carries sticks or other objects for you, this training will help you harness your dog's chasing and fetching abilities and enable you to more accurately predict what it will do. Otherwise, it may only fetch objects when it feels like it. That is not a reliable retriever.

Remember, the more pleasant you make training, the faster your dog will learn.

The Method for a Non-Retriever

If you have a dog that happily chases an object you have thrown but then runs away with it, you will need to use the BAH correction method to stop it in its tracks. Then, if it responds by coming to you, praise it. If it drops the object, throw it again. If your dog continues to run away, do not chase it. Instead, conduct the training in a preferably narrow area with only one way out that will require your dog to eventually come to you. For example, you may choose a passageway or an area at the side of your house that is blocked off by a fence at one end.

If your dog cannot run away from you due to the confined space, it will eventually have to run to you. As it attempts to run past you, block its path, and then praise it lavishly, acting as if it has done the most wonderful thing imaginable.

The first time you do the training, you will need to repeat this process a few times. Do the same thing several times each day for the next few days. This will teach your dog that the reward (your praise) is better when it returns the object than when it escapes with it. You could also try giving your dog a treat when it gives you the object despite its obvious reluctance to relinquish its new find.

If your dog lies down or refuses to go after the object during training, restrain the dog by either tying it with a lead to something stationary or placing it in a crate where it can watch you play fetch with the object. Repeat this process several times a week over a period of a few weeks. Most dogs will want to copy you and retrieve the article themselves.

TEACHING YOUR DOG TO FIND

As we mentioned earlier, dogs have a much more refined sense of smell than we do, which plays an important role in teaching your dog to find. Humans have about five million olfactory cells, compared to two hundred million in a German shepherd. (The exact number varies by breed.) With this physical makeup, the dog relies more heavily on its sense of smell than other senses. For example, if you were to place a stuffed tiger in your living room, your dog might see it and perceive it as a real threat, which would send a message to the brain to react. Most likely, your dog would growl and bark at the stuffed animal. However, once it had a chance to sniff the object, it would realize that it is not alive and therefore not a threat. While its eyes said danger, its sense of smell proved otherwise. At that point, the dog would probably ignore the stuffed tiger altogether.

The Method

Teaching your dog to find can be very beneficial. You can ask for your dog's help to find items you have lost, such as keys, wallets, even money. Before beginning this exercise, make sure your dog is a reliable retriever.

To teach your dog how to find objects, you will need a small wallet or glove that has your scent on it and a screw-top jar with diced meat or an otherwise easy-to-handle food your dog enjoys. Place your dog in a sit/stay position, then walk in a direct line about 25 paces in front of your dog. Take some food out of the jar, and place it on the ground.

Return to your dog and say SEEK over and over, gently leading it toward the spot where you left the food. Once your dog has found the food, allow it to eat it, and praise your dog as it does. Repeat this process several times, each time extending the distance until you are eventually out of sight; for example, behind a tree or hedge. By going out of the dog's sight temporarily, you will teach it to start using its nose. Since it cannot see where you placed the food, it will start sniffing the ground to find it. Practice this method with your dog first on lead and then off lead once your dog is reliably performing the exercise.

After your dog has found the hidden food several times, start from the beginning again, placing the food about twenty-five paces away from your dog and then gradually moving farther away until you are placing it out of sight again. This time, place the wallet or glove with your scent on it next to the food and get your dog to pick up the item after it is finished eating the food. Praise your dog lavishly as it picks up the item, and then run backward towards the spot where you first began the exercise. You don't have to go all the way back to that point, as long as your dog learns to bring the item to you over some distance. Continue this until your dog is reliably finding the food and bringing you the object of its own volition.

Once this happens, repeat the exercise again but this time without leaving any food next to the object. Follow your dog to the spot; as soon as it starts to look for the food, command SEEK and make sure that the dog picks up the article. If your dog does not pick up the item, kick the object with your foot. A reliable fetcher will go after the item. Again, praise your dog and then run backwards. This time reward your dog with the food when it returns to you with the object. Be sure to keep any unused food in the jar; otherwise your dog could become distracted looking for its treat. Use the BAH correction if the dog starts sniffing for more food and ignoring the purpose of the exercise. Praise your dog for bringing the article to you, take the object, and then feed the dog a treat immediately. Repeat this five more times; then discontinue using the food altogether.

Conduct this exercise each day for the next several days, each time phasing out the food by the end of the training session when your dog is enthusiastically seeking out the object.

Be sure not to tire your dog with too many SEEK exercises. About four a day are sufficient after the introductory training session; any more and your dog could consider the exercise tedious.

After a few days, change the pattern. Instead of moving away from the dog, command it to walk correctly by your side, and carefully drop the object (without your dog seeing it) while you are walking. You need to teach your dog to use its nose to find the object. That way, when you really lose something, your dog will have a better chance of finding it for you.

You will need to cover a reasonable distance, following a horseshoe-shaped path from one end to the other. Once you reach the end, do an about-turn and send your dog back in the direction from which you just came, commanding it to SEEK.

Continue this exercise over a period of days until your dog consistently seeks out the objects you have dropped. Change the walking pattern and the objects from time to time to teach your dog to find all types of things for you.

By teaching your dog first to follow the scent of food and then your own scent, it will learn to find a variety of objects and can progress easily to finding other people simply by following the scent.

CASE STUDY

We can vividly remember the day our daughter, Donna (who was only four years old at the time), asked if she could buy an ice cream from the van that regularly came to our street on the weekends.

We gave her the last coin we had on us at the time, and she ran off happily to buy a cone. In no time she was back crying. The coin had fallen out of her hand and was now lost in the long grass at the side of the road.

We tried looking but to no avail. It was a small coin, and the area was vast. We decided to give our dog Monty a go at finding the money, but we did not hold out much hope considering how small the coin was. We allowed him to sniff Donna's arm and then commanded, "Seek." He bounded away, sniffing the ground as he went.

We watched as he circled around, pushing his nose deep into the lush grass. Then suddenly he appeared to have given up. He returned to us, wagging his tail.

"Never mind, feller," we said. "You tried your best." He nuzzled his nose against our legs and spat out a small coin.

Donna was delighted and ran to catch the ice cream van. Monty was given a nice big juicy bone for his wonderful efforts.

TEACHING YOUR DOG TO TRACK

This is another skill that requires your dog to use its exceptional sense of smell. A dog has an innate ability to decipher and follow particular scents; you just need to teach your dog how to harness that power.

The Method

Since dogs love to sniff things, it's relatively easy to teach a dog to track. You will need a screw top jar with some diced meat or otherwise easy-to-handle food inside. The food will be used as a reward for your dog when it finds you during this exercise. You will also need a firm fitting leather collar or a tracking harness (available from your local pet shop) and a twenty-foot long soft webbing lead or a horse lunging lead (available from equestrian suppliers).

Ask a friend to accompany you to a large field or park. Have your assistant hold your dog as you walk a short distance and hide. Then have your assistant let your dog lead it to where you are hiding. Your dog should run to the spot where you stood before you hid, put its nose to the ground and follow your scent to your hiding place. Praise your dog when it finds you, and give it a treat.

Repeat this exercise several times over the next few weeks, several times a day, three to four times per week, increasing the distance and varying the time that your assistant waits before allowing your dog to find you. Once your dog is proficient at finding you, have your friend hide. You can try this with other friends and even people the dog does not know. Never let the dog run free to track. This exercise must always be carried out on lead, just in case the dog runs off and gets lost.

CASE STUDY

A somewhat serious situation was averted by the tracking ability of a lovable mutt called Casey. She was a crossbred bearded collie-standard poodle who belonged to Simon, a friend of ours, and she was a wonderful tracking dog.

A three-year-old girl named Sara had become lost in the wild in Simon's neighborhood. When Simon heard about the missing girl, he decided to see if Casey might be able to help with the search. Simon had Sara's mother fetch the pajamas her daughter had worn the night before. Simon held the garments to Casey's nose, and the dog immediately began to whine.

"Track," Simon commanded, and the dog calmly put her nose to the ground and began sniffing it, circling and doubling back until she appeared to pick up on a scent. She carried on like this for about an hour until eventually she led Simon to what appeared to be an old mine site.

Casey now became very excited. Suddenly, the dog stopped and peered into the mouth of a mine shaft and began wagging its tail and barking excitedly.

Simon knelt down beside Casey and looked into the darkened shaft. As his eyes became accustomed to the dark, he could see a frail little figure huddled against a wall. It was Sara. She just sat there, staring into his eyes. Simon told her that her parents would be with her soon and ran back to tell the search party where the little girl was. He later found out that the family had searched the same area earlier to no avail.

Soon, Sara and her family were reunited, and the little girl made a full recovery from her trauma.

Casey was called upon many times after that day to assist local police, until they finally obtained their own tracking dogs.

TEACHING YOUR DOG TO DISTINGUISH SCENTS

While tracking may be an easy skill to learn, teaching your dog to distinguish scents is one of the most difficult training exercises. Dogs normally do this as a matter of course, but on an instinctive level only. It will be difficult to communicate to the dog what you want it to do because you cannot demonstrate the action.

For example, if you correct your dog for picking up the wrong article, the dog could interpret the correction to mean you do not want it to pick up anything. You will need to be very careful with how you correct and reward your dog during the training. But if you follow these steps, you should be able to communicate exactly what you want without confusing your dog.

The Method

Teaching your dog to retrieve is a prerequisite for this exercise. The key training aid is a pair of recently worn socks that are rolled into a ball. Don't worry if they've been on your feet; the more they smell, the more your dog will love them.

With your dog sitting beside you, throw the socks on the ground about six feet away. Command your dog with the word FIND (or something similar of your choosing). Just remember to keep it brief and always use the same command.

If your dog is already a reliable fetcher, it should easily pick up the socks and bring them to you. If it refuses, pick up the socks yourself and throw them a bit farther, repeating the command FIND. You can also try to excite your dog by shaking the socks before throwing them, again commanding FIND (or whatever word you have chosen).

Once your dog is reliably picking up the socks and bringing them to you, place the dirty socks in the middle of a pile of clean or new socks. Command your dog once again to FIND the socks, praising it as soon as it sniffs at the right pair of socks. Don't say anything if it sniffs the wrong pair. If you correct the dog, it could think you want it to stop sniffing the pile entirely.

Some exuberant breeds will just dash out and grab the first thing they see. If your dog brings back the wrong socks, do not correct it. Just remove the pair it has brought you and try again. Praise your dog but only when it picks up the right pair of socks.

The idea behind using the socks is to remove all doubts from the dog's mind as to what you want it to do. The strong smell from the dirty socks will help your dog learn the objective very quickly.

Once your dog is regularly performing this exercise correctly, use some pieces of wood instead of socks. Take one piece of wood and place it either in your belt close to your skin or in another position where it will pick up your scent, such as up your sleeve. Leave it there for about two to three minutes; then throw the "scented" piece of wood on the ground and have your dog fetch it.

Repeat the exercise using the scented piece of wood; then place another, but this time unscented, piece of wood on the ground next to the scented piece and in front of the dog. Then place another and later another. Always use tongs to place the unscented wood on the ground. Do not add a new piece of unscented wood until your dog has picked the correct (scented) one out of the pile. Keep adding pieces of wood until you have about six pieces on the ground and your dog is selecting the right piece each time you try the exercise.

Initially during training, no one should touch any of the wood except you. This will no longer matter once your dog has learned to do the exercise correctly.

Repeat this exercise regularly over the next few days, several times during each session. Vary the types of objects you use; for example, try some pieces of leather or small pieces of metal pipe (around four to five inches long).

TEACHING YOUR DOG TO DROP AT A DISTANCE

In order to successfully command your dog to DROP when it is some distance away, you will first need to get your dog used to dropping exactly where it is when it hears the command. Having originally learned the DROP command when it was by your side, your dog will probably try to walk toward you when commanded. It associates DROP with not only being in a lowered position but also close to you.

To help your dog make the transition from dropping beside you to dropping at a distance, start the exercise standing close to your dog with it facing you in a standing position and on lead. If you want, you can allow your dog to walk around on the lead.

Use the DROP command while giving your dog a hand signal. The exact hand signal can be your choice as long as you use the same one consistently. It should include a slight movement of your right hand away from your body, then a slight movement upward, followed by another down again pointing at the ground. If your dog fails to respond to your command to DROP, correct it by growling BAH.

If your dog refuses to drop, step forward as soon as you signal with your right hand and gently push your dog into a drop position with your left hand, praising it as you do. Then step back to where you started. Allow ten seconds to pass; then say FREE and encourage your dog to move.

Repeat the "dropping at a distance" exercise several times. Then extend the distance between you and your dog until your dog is dropping up to fifty feet away. If the dog refuses to respond to your command and does not drop immediately, move quickly toward it and place it in the drop position. Be careful not to frighten your dog and cause it to run away. If that happens, do not chase it. Instead freeze and correct it with the BAH word.

Once the dog realizes what you want, it will stop moving and will eventually adopt the drop position every time you say DROP. Although you will initially conduct this exercise with your dog on lead, move to off-lead training once the dog is doing the exercise reliably.

TEACHING YOUR DOG TRICKS

Learning tricks will be a welcome break for your dog from the more regimented obedience exercises. Dogs love learning tricks, but you will need to have some control over your dog in order to teach it correctly.

You will need three training aids to teach your dog tricks quickly: 1) a tennis ball, 2) food for a treat, and 3) praise, all things that dogs love. You decide whether the tennis ball or food will excite the dog enough to perform the trick required. Praise, on the other hand, should be an integral part of each exercise. It's the only way your dog will know that it is doing what you want.

When teaching your dog tricks, make sure not to overwork it. Most dogs will only perform an exercise happily four or five times in a row before it is considered work. Dog training should be fun for you and your dog.

Sitting Up

Some dogs, especially smaller ones, will not need much encouragement to adopt this position. But remember, most long-bodied breeds, such as the dachshund, will probably never master the trick. With dogs such as these, concentrate on other tricks instead.

Some of the larger breeds will find sitting up a bit more challenging physically, but they can master it with some patience and perseverance on your part.

Find a non-slip area for your dog to sit. Then lift both of its front paws over your arm and attempt to balance its body fully over its hindquarters, saying BEG as you do. Once it is balanced on your arm, try to get the dog to balance itself without using your arm as a brace, even if just for a few seconds. As soon as it does, praise the dog, and allow it to return to the sitting position.

Repeat this three or four times over the next several days or until your dog sits up without assistance.

If necessary, food can be used to entice your dog to perform this trick. Simply hold the food above its head once it is in the sit position, keeping the food just out of its reach. Give your dog the food as soon as it balances on its hind quarters for a few seconds; then, allow it to move out of the position by using the FREE command.

Bowing

This is a simple trick to teach your dog and a real crowd pleaser. Place your dog on lead in a standing position; gently press on its shoulders with your right hand, saying BOW as you gently place your left hand under its belly, preventing it from going into a full drop position. With daily practice, your dog will quickly learn to do this adorable trick.

PLAYING DEAD

Have you or someone you know ever been moved to tears watching a movie in which the canine hero is wounded and lying on its side, seeming to die? The dog was only playing dead, a trick you can teach your dog to do easily as long as it reliably obeys the drop/stay exercise. Kneel down beside your dog while it is in the drop position and gently grip it under the chin with your right hand. Then, holding its head firmly, roll your dog onto its side.

Roll your dog to the side to which it is already leaning. For example, if your dog is leaning on its left hip, roll it that way. As you start rolling your dog, say PLAY DEAD and then praise it when it has rolled over onto its side. Use the BAH correction if it tries to resist you. Have your dog stay in this position for a minute, and then say FREE, giving it lots of praise.

Repeat this exercise daily so that your dog will do the trick reliably whenever you want it to, including times when distractions, such as other people or dogs, are present.

CRAWLING

This is another fairly simple trick to teach a dog that has reliably learned the drop exercises. If you have a dog that you plan to trial in competitions, delay teaching this exercise until its show days are over. The danger in teaching this exercise to a competing dog is that it could become confused between the drop/stay and crawl exercises and may start crawling forward instead of staying during a competition.

To teach your dog how to crawl, place it on lead and in a drop position. Gather the lead up short in your right hand, while keeping your left hand on the dog's back to prevent it from standing up. To crawl correctly, your dog will need to lift its shoulders slightly; be sure to allow for this.

Gently tug the lead toward you and move slightly, encouraging your dog to move toward as you say CRAWL. Praise your dog for even a slight attempt at moving forward. This trick will take a lot of practice. While teaching your dog, stand in a balanced position with your legs slightly apart. Make sure you do not place any weight on your dog's back. Your hand is there only to prevent your dog from standing up, not to push it down. Practice the crawl regularly, but no more than four times a day.

WEAVING

All types of breeds love this trick, and it is a very easy one to teach your dog. In your right hand, hold a three-foot lead attached to your dog and either a tennis ball or your dog's favorite toy. Then, with your dog in the normal walking position on your left side and both of you facing forward, hold your legs apart and pass the lead between them in a straight line, leading the dog

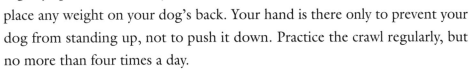

through as you do. Keep the lead and toy in your left hand, and say THROUGH.

Let your dog see the ball or toy, but keep the object just out of the dog's reach as you pass it back through your legs. Once the dog has gone through your legs, take your next step, making sure your dog passes between your legs again as you do. This exercise should be done slowly at first; otherwise, you and your dog could end up in a big tangle on the ground. Just keep practicing over a period of a week or two, several times a day, three to four days per week, taking care not to let your dog tire of the exercise.

JUMPING THROUGH A HOOP

Teaching your dog to jump through a hoop is really just an extension of the original jumping exercise. The only difference is that your dog will have to jump through a hoop instead of over an object. This exercise should only require a small adjustment on your dog's part.

You can use either a hula hoop or an old bicycle rim and your dog's favorite ball or toy. Start off by holding the hoop close to the ground and the object on the opposite side, so that the dog has to jump through the hoop to get to it. Say THROUGH as the dog jumps, and praise it as it completes the exercise. Utter the BAH correction if your dog tries to get to the object by going around the hoop.

Practice makes perfect with this exercise. Keep adjusting the height of the hoop until your dog is jumping comfortably through it every time. Food can be used instead of the ball or toy. Once again, check with your local breed club to determine a safe height for your dog to jump.

JUMPING OVER THE OWNER'S BACK

This is another variation on the original jumping exercise, except that this time your dog will be jumping over your back. Ask someone your dog already knows to help you with this trick.

Have your helper hold your dog on lead while you crouch on the ground on all fours. Be prepared for the possibility that your dog could interpret you in this position as an invitation to play. If so, have your friend correct your dog with the BAH word. You will be in too low a position to be dominant and may be ignored by your dog. Once you are in position, have your assistant say OVER and run toward you with the dog on a shortened lead.

At this stage, your dog may just jump onto your back, but with a good correction from your assistant and a snap of the lead as he or she runs past you, the dog will go where it should. Have your assistant repeat this exercise several times, each time giving the command OVER and praising the dog as it jumps over your back.

Once your dog understands what you want, and with plenty of practice, eventually all you will have to do is place your dog in a sit position, crouch down on all fours, and then say the command OVER to get your dog to go sailing over your back.

You can teach your dog to jump higher just by raising your height slightly, but remember not to ask a dog to jump higher than it should.

CARRYING OBJECTS

When teaching your dog to carry things, consider the shape and size, as well as the weight, of the object. Also, keep your dog's height and size in mind.

The wrong shaped or sized object can interfere with your dog's movements, perhaps causing it to bump into things while walking. Our dogs carry brooms, buckets, baskets, briefcases, newspapers and telephone directories, to name just a few things, but we had to introduce these items gradually, after first teaching them to carry much smaller and lighter items. This way they were able to adjust to carrying heavier articles.

Start by teaching your dog to hold a rolled newspaper in its mouth. Face your dog and take two steps back while encouraging your dog to take a few steps toward you. Say BRING as you do. If your dog already fetches things, you won't have much trouble teaching it this exercise. If the dog won't hold the newspaper, go back to teaching it to hold a soft item first, as described earlier under "Teaching a Natural Retriever."

Once your dog will carry a newspaper successfully, progress slowly to different items such as small books, soft toys and your dog's own lead (folded, so that it does not entangle the dog's legs).

As long as you do not rush this training, your dog will learn to enjoy carrying objects for you.

DOING THE SHOPPING

This used to be a popular trick, but there are dangers in allowing your dog to wander off by itself, such as being hit by traffic, or simply because an unaccompanied dog without a leash is illegal in most communities. However, it can be extremely useful if your dog is doing television or movie work.

The Method

We trained our dog to do the shopping by first teaching it to take a basket from one person to the next. We do not provide instructions on how to get a dog to actually go shopping since this is probably impractical for those of us who live in large cities with chain grocery stores that have regulations prohibiting dogs inside and due to the reasons mentioned above.

Select a well-shaped shopping basket that your dog can hold comfortably and that will not bump against its chest when walking. Put in some empty packets or very lightweight groceries. You can increase the weight later, once your dog learns to carry the weight of the basket.

Teach your dog to carry the basket by putting it in its mouth, waiting a few seconds, and then saying GIVE. If you have already taught your dog to hold items in its mouth, you will probably not need a command for this part of the exercise.

Once you are sure your dog will continue to hold the basket, walk backwards, encouraging it to bring the basket to you by saying BRING as you move away from your dog. Eventually, your dog will recognize the word BRING as the command for this exercise.

CASE STUDY

Although not practical in most communities, we do know of a man whose Labrador named Bessie did the shopping for him.

Bessie always used to accompany her owner when he went to the store, carrying the shopping basket for him to the butcher and grocery stores and then back home again.

When her owner became too sick to go out, Bessie pestered the man with constant barking. Since the dog knew the way to the stores and back, he eventually gave her a note, the basket, and some money and let her go on her own.

Knowing Bessie by sight, the local butcher and grocer greeted the dog when she arrived. They each read the notes from the owner, put the required items in the basket, took the payment and sent the dog on her way. When Bessie finished her tasks, she went back home to her owner.

CATCHING A FRISBEE

The easiest way to teach your dog to catch a Frisbee is to follow these three steps:

Step 1: Place your dog in a sit position, while you stand about six feet in front of it. Throw some small morsels of food to your dog, saying CATCH at the same time.

Step 2: Once your dog is successfully catching the food morsels, use a tennis ball instead. This time, throw the ball so it can catch it with its mouth. Praise the dog as soon as it catches the ball. Keep practicing over the next few days, making sure you do not practice any exercise more than five times in a session.

Step 3: Once your dog has accomplished Step Two, introduce the Frisbee. This time, place your dog in a sit position about ten feet away. Throw the Frisbee so it flies just a very short distance above the dog's head and say CATCH. Repeat this four or five times, trying to finish the session with your dog actually catching the Frisbee.

Bringing Another Dog in on a Lead

Before trying this exercise, make sure your dog can fetch its lead. You will also need another dog that is compatible with your own.

Place your dog's lead on the ground. Show it where the lead is and say BRING, asking it to bring the lead to you.

Have your dog bring the lead to you a few times, and then attach the lead to an article such as a rolled-up towel or a small blanket. Now, ask your dog to BRING its lead to you, only this time you will need to encourage the dog to drag the extra weight by praising it the instant it appears to feel the extra burden.

Once your dog has mastered this, attach the lead to the friendly dog that is helping you, or have another person hold the lead, and get your dog to bring this person to you. Eventually, try this trick with different people and dogs.

Continue to practice this exercise a few times a week, several times each training session, until your dog performs the trick reliably.

By practicing the training techniques in the preceding chapters, you can have a rewarding relationship throughout your dog's life. At times, however, life circumstances can change. The next chapter helps you deal with changes in your life and that of your dog.

SECTION SIX

Special Circumstances

In this section, we will discuss how to handle special circumstances, such as introducing your dog to other pets in your household, what to do with your dog when you are on vacation, and how to care for older animals and those with special needs. By combining what you have already learned about how dogs think and learn with the training techniques covered in this book, you will be prepared to foster a healthy and rewarding relationship with your dog throughout both of your lives. If you require assistance with an issue not addressed in this chapter, check with a Bark Busters therapist in your area. You can find a therapist by visiting www.BarkBusters.com or calling one of the numbers in the Appendix.

CHILDREN AND DOGS

To a dog, children have no pack status; as a result, dogs will not respect them nor accept their authority. Because dogs relate to children as if they are puppies or playthings, a child under 12 years of age should never discipline a dog.

If a child were to do so, the dog could react by correcting the child for over-stepping his or her authority. This scolding could take the form of a simple snap of the teeth or escalate to a full attack, depending on the dog's tempera-ment, the child's reaction, and how severe the dog may have considered the initial indiscretion by the child.

Many dogs lose their lives because parents do not understand how a dog's mind works. The horror of a dog snapping at a child is more than most par-ents can bear, when the dog was only acting according to its innate form of justice and was correcting the child for overstepping the boundaries of pack hierarchy.

The whole process may seem vicious and barbaric, but we must remem-ber that this is how dogs discipline each other, according to pack law. A per-son hits with his hands; a dog hits with its mouth. This is another reason why you should never try to correct a dog using physical punishment. If you do, your child might emulate your actions, and the dog, having no respect for the child's authority, could try to correct the child for being insolent.

In the wild, dogs protect their own pups from other pack members that might consider the puppies to be a threat to their own status. As such, we need to clearly demonstrate to our dogs that our children are precious to us and that dogs should not step out of line. The following steps can help establish your children's pack status in the dog's mind. Be sure to correct your dog with the BAH command if it disobeys:

- Make sure children always precede dogs and puppies through door-ways, up and down stairs and when going from room to room.
- No dog or puppy should be allowed to steal food from a child or otherwise act in a dominant manner; for example, jumping up on the child or pushing him or her out of the way.
- Dogs should not be allowed to snap or growl at an approaching child and should be corrected immediately for doing so.

If you have a puppy, you can try setting up a carefully controlled situation in which your child runs around and plays to excite the dog. As soon as the dog indicates its intention to jump up or otherwise play roughly with the child, growl and clap your hands while instructing your child to freeze.

Under no circumstances should the child correct the puppy for its actions. If the training is executed as explained, the puppy eventually will accept the child's reaction of freezing as a subliminal correction, associating it with the correction it received from you and instinctively knowing this is how a more dominant dog would behave. If a child is encouraged to discipline a puppy for its bad behavior, problems could occur when the puppy, growing at a faster rate than the child, reaches maturity. In the dog's eyes, the child will still have no authority, and the matured dog is now likely to correct the child, this time with the potential to cause considerably more harm to the child.

Some dogs understandably become excited around children because they run around and scream, compared to adults who generally move much more calmly. A child who is permitted to roughhouse with a family dog could be corrected by the dog when it has had enough of the rough treatment. Also, children visiting the house could be in danger of being bitten. A dog may have the impression that children mean pain, and it could attempt a preemptive strike.

Always supervise your children when they are with a dog. While dogs can be taught to respect children, even the most well-trained dog might revert to the ways of the pack if left unattended with a child. Leaving your child and your dog alone is like leaving two young children together. More than likely, they will eventually get into some dispute, and the dog will fight back the only way it knows how, with its teeth. Snapping or even biting a child is, to the dog, nothing more than smacking the child, which your child may have actually done first to the dog.

Not only are we responsible for the behavior of our dogs around children, but we are also responsible for the behavior of our children around dogs. Unfortunately for many dogs, children do not realize the kind of pain they can inflict by stepping or jumping on, kicking, squeezing, pinching, or pulling on parts of a dog's body. Even the most well-tempered dog will have its breaking point. We must teach children that dogs are not toys, but rather living things that can experience pain. Instruct your child never to disturb an animal that is resting or sleeping, eating a meal, playing, or chewing a favorite object.

CASE STUDY

Clancy, an eighteen-month-old Siberian husky, was an adorable and gentle creature, until he went to live with a family that had an energetic three-year-old boy.

Clancy was six months old when he was purchased from a breeder as a pet for the boy. For many months, he tolerated the child's rough advances: the young boy would hit Clancy in his face and stand on Clancy's toes. In the beginning, Clancy would try to move away when he saw the boy coming. He looked to his owners to do something, but the boy was their only child, and in their eyes, he could do no wrong. Clancy obviously realized that he was a plaything at the child's mercy. If the pack leaders were not going to deal with the problem, the dog would have to take action to protect himself.

The next time the child cornered him, Clancy snapped to warn him to back off. The child, however, was not in the habit of listening to anyone, let alone a dog, and he just kept coming. Clancy knew he would have to take more drastic steps to make the child stop his advances, so he leapt at the child's face and nipped him on the cheek.

> Clancy had hit pay dirt this time: the child screamed and immediately backed off, running to his mother. Clancy was satisfied; he had taught the child a lesson and felt sure the child would not bother him again.
>
> He was right. The next day Clancy was put to sleep at the local animal welfare shelter.

Problems between children and dogs usually occur when a child is between two and five years old, with the majority of dog bites involving children inflicted by either the family dog or one owned by a friend or relative. Even dogs that have been conditioned to a new baby in the house (see "Tips for Expectant Parents" later in this section) may exhibit aggressive behavior toward the child once he or she begins crawling and walking. Your dog may not recognize this mobile creature as the same one that previously was only carried from place to place. Predatory behavior and the dog's strong instinct to hunt small creatures could develop in a dog that previously showed no interest in or aggression toward your child. Keep your dog in the sit/stay position by your side as your child moves about the room, correcting your dog if it tries to move and praising it when it obeys your command to STAY.

Many parents believe they can teach children responsibility by having them take care of a dog. We have lost count of how many times we have heard parents tell their children, "It's your pet, and you must look after him." By all means, children may participate in the care and grooming of their pets but only under strict adult supervision. Parents would not think of asking a child to be responsible for the care of a new baby. Yet, we continually see situations where children are expected to be responsible for a creature that is agile, difficult to understand, and can easily outsmart them.

Dally Says™ is a child-safety video produced by Bark Busters to provide a fun way to teach children how to behave around dogs and how to avoid being bitten. You may purchase it from your local Bark Busters therapist.

DOGS AND VISITORS

Interactions between visitors and your dog should also be monitored. Bring your dog into the room only after the visitors have settled in. They may offer your dog a treat, but have them drop it on the ground for the dog to eat. Walk your dog on lead near the visitors, and then take it to its kennel or another room where it will be comfortable. This will create less excitement and anxiety toward visitors, and your dog will associate visitors with something pleasant, as opposed to something that creates anxiety. As we mentioned earlier, aggression problems in dogs can stem from being treated roughly by visitors.

TIPS FOR EXPECTANT PARENTS

Many expectant parents who were comfortable with their dogs before pregnancy become very anxious about what they should do with their dog or puppy when the new baby arrives. The process of making your dog comfortable and well behaved around the new baby will require some work on your part long before the big day arrives, but it can be done confidently and with relative ease.

As early as possible, begin considering what kind of lifestyle changes will be required for your dog. Some people happily allow their dog or puppy to do what it has always done and sleep where it has always slept, while others want to make radical changes, such as no longer allowing a dog to sleep in the bedroom or on the bed. Making this kind of change the night before or day the new baby arrives home is unfair and confusing to the dog. Any such change should be planned and implemented as early as possible. With proper management and training, there should be no problems if the dog is given time to adjust.

Consider, for example, where the baby will sleep and if you will need to bring your baby into your bedroom at night for nursing. An exuberant or out-of-control puppy or dog that is used to sleeping on the bed could present a danger to a newborn baby.

Crating is an ideal way to manage a dog with a new baby in the house. An indoor dog can be crated during the day when you need time with the baby alone, when visitors arrive, or when the baby needs your full attention, such as mealtimes or when you are changing the baby's diaper. (For more on crating, refer to Section Two.)

On the other hand, it is not necessary to change your dog's normal routine, as long as you carefully manage interactions between your dog and the baby and never leave the two alone at any time. A baby wriggling about in his bassinette could be a strong temptation to a dog or puppy.

One way to prepare a dog for the new baby is to give it some understanding of what is to come. We suggest purchasing a doll that cries like a baby and carrying it with you when your dog is around. A baby's cries can excite or panic a dog that is not familiar with the sound. The dog will want to jump up to see what is creating the noise. To a puppy or dog, a crying, wiggling baby in your arms can appear as if you have captured something, enticing your dog to assist you with the catch. If you plan to use a baby carrier, put the doll in the carrier and wear it while you are interacting with your dog. By setting the scene in advance, you will be able to correct any undesirable behavior long before the real baby arrives.

CASE STUDY

A pregnant woman who owned a Rottweiler asked Bark Busters to help her prepare for the day when she would bring the new baby home.

The therapist instructed the expectant mother to wrap up a doll and carry it around the house or place it in a stroller while, at the same time, establishing new rules for her dog.

The woman and therapist were practicing with the mock baby when suddenly the dog jumped up, grabbed the doll out of the woman's arms, and dragged it to the floor.

The dog was corrected for its mistake and quickly learned what was expected.

Also consider how you will dispose of soiled diapers. The scent will prove very enticing to a dog. Don't leave them lying around, and keep your dog well away from them. Dogs have been known to try to get to a diaper when it was still on the baby, which is another important reason why you should never leave a dog and baby alone.

After reading this section, you might panic and think, "Oh, this is too much. We need to find another home for our dog." That is definitely not the case. Your puppy or dog and child can co-exist quite safely, as long as you practice good management and maintain authority over your dog. Like many people, we have raised puppies and children together without any problems whatsoever, and our children have grown up enjoying the companionship of their dogs.

ELDERLY PEOPLE AND DOGS

We often hear stories about well-meaning individuals purchasing a lively puppy for a parent or other elderly person who has recently lost a partner, thinking that a puppy will take his or her mind off the loss. Unfortunately, unless the person is fairly active, this can actually create more stress. A puppy is a huge responsibility that can require as much work as an infant. A better choice for an elderly parent or friend would be a more mature dog, preferably one that is over five years old. Animal shelters have many dogs this age that need a good home.

Look for a dog that is not overactive or too large to handle. All dogs, regardless of age, need some regular exercise, and a large breed could be difficult to walk at first. Older, more mature dogs have long since gotten over their excessive exuberance and generally make great companions.

GOING PLACES

To the Veterinarian's Office

New experiences can be upsetting for some dogs, especially if it is their first time in a car or if the visit is unpleasant; for example, vaccination time. Since regular veterinary visits are critical to protect your dog's health, it is your responsibility to help your dog overcome its fears. If possible, take your dog to the vet for a casual visit before an actual appointment. Either way, always take a treat with you, and ask the veterinarian to give it to your dog. In this way, your dog will associate pleasure, rather than pain, with the vet. Many veterinarian offices have appropriate doggie treats on hand just for this purpose. Gently hold your dog's head and praise it well if it behaves, but correct it immediately using the BAH word if it exhibits any aggression.

To the Grooming Parlor

Some dogs are easily frightened by a visit to the groomer. Again, try to take your dog to visit the groomer before setting an actual appointment. That way, you can make sure you are comfortable with the groomer's ability to handle your particular type of dog and that your dog is familiar with the place and people who will be handling it. Again, take doggie treats for the groomer to give your dog. We recommend at least four casual visits before your dog is first groomed.

If your dog shows aggression or is approached aggressively by other animals at the veterinarian office or grooming parlor, utilize the correction techniques outlined in Section Four.

Do-It-Yourself Grooming

Some dog owners prefer to handle grooming themselves, although longer-haired dogs will probably need to visit a grooming parlor for clipping and coat stripping at some time in their lives.

Among themselves, dogs will allow grooming only by more dominant dogs, which requires you to have established dominance over your dog before attempting to groom it yourself.

To begin grooming, put a lead on your dog. A small dog can be placed on a stable table, while a larger dog will need to be in the stand/stay position. Begin brushing your dog. If it reacts by attempting to bite you or play, freeze the hand that is holding the brush, while growling BAH and checking the lead to let your dog know you do not approve of its behavior. Once your dog stands still and allows you to groom it without wriggling, stop brushing it, praise it lavishly, and then allow your dog to go free.

Extend the grooming time a little with each session. Continue in this manner for a couple of weeks, adding a little extra time each day until your dog looks forward to the experience. You can also examine your puppy: look in its ears and mouth and pick up its paws, correcting any undesirable behavior as you go. This can also help prepare your dog for veterinary examinations.

GOING ON VACATION

There may be times when you need to make arrangements for your dog while you are away for an extended period of time. In these cases, you have several options. You could arrange to have your dog looked after by a trusted family member or neighbor whom the dog knows. You can hire a professional dog sitter to come to your house daily, or you can arrange for your dog to stay at an established boarding facility. Never leave your dog in the hands of inexperienced people, no matter how willing they may be.

Dog-Sitting Services

Professional dog sitters will come to your home to feed and care for your dog while you are away. Some dog sitters will not only care for your dog, but will also pick up your mail, water your plants, and check on home security.

A professionally run service can be invaluable, creating less stress for your dog because it can stay in its own surroundings. Ensure that your yard is secure and that a large water receptacle is accessible to your dog during the day, along with adequate shade and shelter.

Check the credentials of the service provider and ask for references. Also, research the type of insurance they carry. Provide them with all necessary contact numbers and information, including your veterinarian's regular and off-hours numbers and instructions on what to do in the event of a medical emergency.

Supply keys to your home to both the dog sitter and a trusted neighbor in case of fire.

Commercial Boarding

There are numerous boarding establishments in most communities that can provide for your dog's needs, including special dietary requirements. The best way to make sure you choose a good establishment for your dog is to make an appointment to tour the facilities and meet the caregivers. Do not leave your puppy or dog with an establishment that will not let you inspect its facilities beforehand.

Boarding establishments require that dogs have up-to-date vaccinations for distemper, parvovirus, rabies, and kennel cough. Ask your veterinarian about what is required in your area.

ANIMALS WITH SPECIAL NEEDS

Blindness

Blindness, either partial or complete, can be difficult to ascertain when your dog is in familiar surroundings. It may stumble or hesitate but only if you make a change to its environment, such as rearranging the furniture. But with your help, you can help your animal cope with the loss of sight.

Any training you carry out will have to be via sound, making verbal commands a must. By attaching a bell to yourself and to any other person or animal in the household, you can make it easier for your dog to locate you or a companion quickly; its nose will do the rest. Your dog will soon be able to recogn

Always attach a lead whenever you take your dog outside of its natural surroundings.

CASE STUDY

Buddy, a two-year-old bull terrier, was blind. Imagine our surprise when we visited him, only to find the dog and his owner playing a game of catch. Buddy would face his owner and wait for the ball to be thrown. He would hear the ball bounce once and then pounce quickly and with amazing accuracy. With the ball in his mouth, he would bring it to the top of the hill, let it go, and chase it down. You could see the dog concentrating on the sound of the rolling ball, and if he ever momentarily lost track of the ball, his sense of smell would lead him to it.

Teaching a Blind or Visually Impaired Dog to Come When Called

When training a blind or visually impaired dog to come to you, select a safe, fenced area before beginning the exercise. Stand your ground and clap your hands, saying COME in a very high-pitched voice. Remain very still and keep clapping until your dog comes, then praise it. The clapping will allow your dog to hone in on your position.

All lead work and obedience training can be carried out in the same manner as you would for normal-sighted dogs, as long as you have a bell attached to you to enable your dog to find you.

When introducing a visually impaired dog to a new area, do not attempt any off-lead work other than the recall, which can be conducted in a fenced and protected area. Give your dog time to adjust to its new surroundings.

CASE STUDY

It is not always true that visually impaired dogs are totally blind. Sometimes they may just have a visual impairment.

Bark Busters was asked to treat Callan, a black Labrador puppy, for aggression towards other dogs. When we arrived at the house, we noticed that Callan appeared to have a crooked nose.

As we began the normal training procedure, we noticed that Callan was looking to one side of anyone on whom he tried to focus. When he was focused on us, he would look at least a foot to one side of us. We noticed that he did the same with each member of the family.

Not being vets, we weren't sure what the problem was, but it appeared to us that Callan was cross-eyed and possibly saw two of everything. We asked the owners to seek medical attention for their puppy and halted the lesson until a diagnosis was received.

The owners sought several medical opinions and finally received an answer to the mystery. Callan had a rare genetic problem, a condition that gave him double vision and one that was passed on through indiscriminate breeding.

We returned to assist the owners with some special training. We placed a bell on the owner's belt to help Callan identify exactly where the owner was, simply by locating the sound.

Deafness

Our aging bull terrier, Bullseye, was deaf for approximately two years before passing away. We could yell at the top of our voices and he would just ignore us. However, if we clapped in quick succession, he would stop what he was doing and come running. We devised signals for him, and he quickly caught on to what was required of him.

Many hearing-impaired dogs can actually hear clapping because it has a different pitch than voice tones. Some partially deaf dogs hear only very high-pitched sounds and do not respond to lower-pitched tones. High-pitched clapping can be used to get your dog to look in your direction, giving you an opportunity to give the signals required.

Visual aids can be used if a dog is totally deaf and does not respond to clapping. The aids may be in the form of a bright- or light-colored object that is dropped on the ground near the puppy, which tells it to look in your direction.

Put your dog on lead and allow it to stride ahead of you, then drop the visual object in front of the dog where it cannot miss seeing it. Gently tug the lead so your dog turns to look at you. Crouch down and, using appropriate body language, encourage your dog to approach, always using the same hand signal every time.

Praise your dog by gently rubbing its ears, repeating the process several times. With patience, your dog will soon learn to turn and look to see what you want whenever the visual aid is dropped in its path.

The higher-pitched sound emitted by a Bark Busters training pillow can be heard by some dogs that have suffered only partial hearing loss. They also make a great visual aid for deaf dogs. The training pillow also has sufficient weight for a visually impaired dog to feel the impact when it hits the ground.

A flashlight or laser beam can also be used, but special care must be taken. Make sure your dog does not start chasing the beam as a game. Irresponsible or overuse of a light beam can also create obsessive compulsive disorder. Under no circumstances should you shine the beam into or near the eyes of a dog.

The beam is used only to teach your dog to look at you for further instruction. Shine the beam ahead of the dog while it is on lead. Flick the lead to encourage the dog to look at you every time it sees the beam. A flashlight works especially well at night. Turn off the flashlight the instant the puppy looks in your direction.

Senior Dogs

The rate at which dogs age depends on a variety of factors, including breed, size, and their general health. In general, the larger the dog, the faster it will age. Your pet's behavior may change as it grows older. It may remain playful at times, even at an advanced age, but its stamina will decline. Behavior problems that manifest as a dog ages may signal a health issue. Annual veterinarian appointments can help determine if a problem is the result of a medical disorder or simply old age. Many dogs begin to experience loss of sight and hearing as they grow older.

CASE STUDY

As our aging dogs grow feebler, we may one day have the sad task of deciding whether they should be put to sleep. We had to make that decision about our ever-faithful, beloved Gypsy. She had been a very active dog, but not long after her thirteenth birthday she could not walk any more; her spleen had probably ruptured. The veterinarian said he could operate, but there was no guarantee of success. Her age would be against her. With this and the certainty that her quality of life would be worse if she survived, we had her put to sleep. We remained with her, patting her head, and she went to sleep peacefully. It is important that you stay with your dog at this time so it suffers no added stress or anxiety.

A post mortem later showed a huge tumor; Gypsy would not have survived in any case. We believe that when your dog has major difficulties such as being unable to walk, it no longer has a good quality of life. Now a decision must be made, and the owner is the only person who can make it. No one else knows your dog better than you do.

A friend once called us to inform us of the death of his much-loved Doberman, Pontiac. As the conversation ended, he thanked us for our sympathy. Other friends who were not dog lovers could not understand why he was so upset, commenting that it was "only a dog."

"Yes," we said. "It's only a dog. Only one of the most faithful and endearing friends you will ever have."

About the Authors

Sylvia and Danny Wilson have more than fifty years combined experience in addressing dog behavioral issues and training dogs deemed untrainable.

Sylvia was the child in her hometown who everyone called when they had a problem with their dog. Sylvia pioneered the "Difficult Dog Programme," a program designed to train those dogs considered to be untrainable or too aggressive by other trainers. Sylvia then managed an RSPCA shelter where she again implemented the "Difficult Dog Programme." Danny spent many childhood years learning the secrets of how farmers trained their dogs to herd cattle and sheep. Now when Danny visits his hometown, the locals call on him to help them with their dogs. Saddened by the ever-growing number of healthy dogs euthanized for behavioral problems, Sylvia and Danny set out to help humans better understand the canine psyche and, thus, save dogs lives. Together they founded Bark Busters International in 1989, now the world's largest dog training company. Bark Busters Home Dog Training has hundreds of locations throughout the USA and around the world and is still growing.

Sylvia and Danny live in Huskisson, New South Wales, Australia, with their cadre of dogs, three horses, and a pet pigeon, named Sidney. Together they travel the world speaking to groups, small and large, advocating for natural, humane training methods and championing responsible dog ownership to enhance the human-canine bond.

About Bark Busters

Bark Busters, the world's largest dog training company, was started in Australia in 1989 by Sylvia and Danny Wilson, expert dog trainers and authors of many dog training books. Sylvia was the manager of an RSPCA shelter in Australia and studied the behavior and communication methods of dogs for years. She was saddened by the number of dogs she saw being abandoned and euthanized for behavioral problems, which she knew was due to a lack of consistent leadership. This became the basis for creating the unique, natural training techniques and several books that teach owners how to train their dogs through the use of voice tones and body language, all geared toward putting the owner in control through effective leadership. These dog-friendly, non-physical techniques have propelled Bark Busters' phenomenal growth—now the world's largest dog training company with hundreds of offices in 8 countries, including locations in more than 40 U.S. states.

With the experience of training hundreds of thousands of dogs worldwide, Bark Busters dog behavioral therapists are renowned authorities in correcting dog behavior. The Bark Busters natural training system can successfully train any dog, even a puppy, by leveraging the same communications methods —body language and voice control—that dogs follow as part of their instinctual pack mentality. About 80 percent of Bark Busters clients require only one two-hour home visit from a licensed dog behavioral therapist, if owners continue with follow-up exercises just 10 to15 minutes a day for several weeks. All training takes place right in the home where the problems generally occur. In every market where Bark Busters is established, a majority of veterinarians familiar with its techniques recommend the company's services. And Bark Busters is the only international dog training company that offers a worldwide written lifetime guaranteed.

As a world leader in natural home dog training, Bark Busters and its global network of dog behavioral therapists are championing responsible dog ownership to enhance enjoyment of our canine friends and reduce the possibility of abuse and euthanasia of companion dogs.

How to Find a Bark Busters Dog Behavioral Therapist

In the USA
visit www.BarkBusters.com or call 1 877 500 BARK (2275).

In Australia
visit www.BarkBusters.com.au or call 1 800 067 710.

In New Zealand
visit www.BarkBusters.co.nz or call 0 800 167 710.

In Canada
visit www.BarkBusters.ca or call 1 866 418 4584.

In the UK
visit www.BarkBusters.co.uk or call 0 808 100 4071.

In Israel
visit www.BarkBusters.co.il or call 1 800 21 31 31.

In Japan
visit www.BarkBusters.co.jp or call 0 120 272 109.

In Taiwan
visit www.BarkBusters.com.tw or call 0 800 287 837.

Index